Herbert Puchta, Jeff Stranks
and Peter Lewis-Jones

English in Mind

Second edition

Workbook 4

CAMBRIDGE
UNIVERSITY PRESS

Welcome section

① Past tense review

Underline the correct option.

I [1] *watched* / *was watching* Rain Man on DVD the other day when a part of the dialogue really [2] *caught* / *was catching* my attention. In fact I [3] *was* / *had been* so surprised that I rewound the film to make sure I [4] *was hearing* / *had heard* correctly. In the film, the character Raymond Babbitt, who is autistic, claimed that Qantas was the only airline that [5] *never had* / *had never had* a crash. I [6] *went* / *had gone* online to check out this fact.

Apparently it wasn't 100% true. At the time of the making of the film, Qantas [7] *had had* / *was having* eight crashes but they [8] *were all being* / *had all been* propeller planes, not jets. I also [9] *found* / *had found* out that all airlines (except for Qantas, of course) [10] *took* / *were taking* this line out of the film when they [11] *were showing* / *showed* it on flights at the time.

② *be used to* + gerund vs *used to* + infinitive

Complete the sentences with the correct form of the verb in brackets.

1 My dad used to _____*be*_____ (be) a doctor but he retired.

2 I'm not used to _____ (get up) early.

3 When I was a teenager, I used to _____ (ride) my bike everywhere.

4 When I first arrived in Brazil I wasn't used to _____ (kiss) people when I met them.

5 My grandmother used to _____ (tell) us great bedtime stories.

6 He's a pilot so he's used to _____ (work) long hours.

7 She used to _____ (be) my friend but we had an argument.

8 After two years in Italy, I'm used to _____ (drink) strong coffee.

③ Personality adjectives

Read each definition and write the correct word at the end of each sentence.

| bit bossy considerate ~~insensitive~~ bad-tempered |
| imaginative sensible independent ambitious |

1 Tom doesn't think about other people's feelings and emotions. __*insensitive*__

2 She has a lot of good ideas and is very creative. _____

3 Greg always does the practical thing: never does anything silly. _____

4 Ann likes to tell others what to do all the time. _____

5 He likes to do things on his own. _____

6 Claire wants a lot from life. _____

7 She thinks about others and how they might be feeling. _____

8 My boss is never in a good mood, he's always angry about something. _____

B

1 should / should have

Complete the sentences with *should(n't)* and the correct form of the verb in brackets.

1 If you're not feeling well, you
___should lie___ (lie) down for a while.

2 You _____ (tell) him yourself.
Then he wouldn't have been so upset
when he found out from Milly.

3 It's really hot out there today. You
_____ (take) a hat with you if
you don't want to get sunburnt.

4 I'm not surprised he had an accident.
He _____ (take) the car out
when there was so much snow.

5 I think we _____ (bring) more
food with us. I'm starting to get really
hungry.

6 You _____ (say) that. Now
she's crying!

7 You _____ (be) careful what
you say to Don. He's very sensitive.

8 You _____ (watch) this film
on your own. It's really scary.

2 Problems

Complete the text with the missing words.

Whenever a big problem comes
¹ ___up___ it's always a good idea to think
it ² _____ for a while, and try to work
it ³ _____ on your own. If you still
can't make your mind ⁴ _____ about
what to do, then you might like to talk it
⁵ _____ with a friend. If that doesn't
make the problem go ⁶ _____ ,
then perhaps you should try and sleep
⁷ _____ it and come ⁸ _____ to it
in the morning. If in the morning you still
don't know what to do then maybe you
should just forget about it all together.
Some problems aren't meant to be solved.

3 wish

Write sentences about what these people might
be wishing.

1 I ate so much and now I feel ill.
I wish I hadn't eaten so much.

2 I just haven't got enough time to do everything.
_____

3 Why can't it be Saturday?
_____

4 I really wanted to see that film, but it's not on at
the cinema any more.
_____

5 I worry about everything. It gets really annoying.
_____

6 I gave that dog my hamburger and now it's
following me all the way home.
_____

7 Why didn't I tell the truth? Now I'm in really
big trouble.
_____

8 I wonder what she's thinking. I'd love to know.
_____

4 Friends

Match the two parts of the sentences.

Friends forever – a declaration of friendship

1 I will always stand   a on you. Your secrets
are safe with me.

2 I will never tell   b out or argue about
anything.

3 I will always stick   c up for you when
others are being
mean.

4 I will never let   d on well forever.

5 We will never fall   e by you, no matter
what you do.

6 We will get   f you down. I'll always
be by your side.

C

1 Present perfect and future passives

Write the sentences in the passive voice.

1 They've announced an exciting new reality show.

   An exciting new reality show has been announced.

2 They'll call the show *Jail Break*.

   ....

   ....

3 They've chosen ten contestants to spend three weeks in a prison.

   ....

   ....

4 They'll ask the contestants to do various tasks.

   ....

   ....

5 The public will nominate contestants to leave the prison.

   ....

   ....

6 They'll crown the last contestant to leave 'King of the Prison.'

   ....

   ....

2 Future predictions

Complete the sentences so that they are true about you.

In the next ten years ...

1 I'm not likely ....

2 I won't ....

3 I'll probably ....

4 I might ....

5 I probably won't ....

6 I'll ....

3 Crimes

What crimes are these people planning? Choose from the words in the box.

> vandalism ~~burglary~~ shoplifting
> pick-pocketing arson joyriding

1 They're going on holiday tomorrow so the house will be empty for a week.
   ...*burglary*...

2 Make sure you wear a coat with big pockets to put lots of things in. ....

3 If you put your hand in and out quickly, they don't notice anything. ....

4 There's an old building by the park with loads of windows we can break.

   ....

5 Are you sure you know how to drive this car? ....

6 Just make sure there's no one in the building when you set fire to it. ....

4 Getting into trouble

Complete with the words in the box.

> ~~got~~ caught committing sent
> do breaking put doing pay

OK, so you've done it a few times and always [1] ...*got*... away with it.

You know you're [2] .... something wrong but you're not really [3] .... any crime, are you? Wrong! Shoplifting is a crime that the police take very seriously. And one day you will get [4] .... Then what? Well, that depends. You may have to [5] .... a heavy fine or [6] .... community service. Get caught again and you'll be [7] .... on probation. Carry on after that and there's a good chance you'll be [8] .... to prison. Shoplifting is serious. [9] .... the law is not a joke!

D

1 Modals of deduction (past)

Rewrite the sentences with a modal of deduction.

1   Tim didn't know your secret. I'm sure he didn't tell Olivia.
    He can't have told Olivia.

2   It's a real antique. I bet he paid a lot for that.

    _____

3   I'm not sure if I paid or not. I can't remember.

    _____

4   She's not talking to me. Maybe I said something to upset her.

    _____

5   You live next door to the crime scene. I'm sure you heard something.

    _____

2 make / let / be allowed to

Complete the dog's thoughts with *(not) let, make* or *(not) be allowed to*.

1   They only *let* me into the house on my birthday. That's only once a year!

2   I _____ chase the cat and they get really cross if I do.

3   They _____ me eat dog food, even though it's really disgusting.

4   They _____ me watch TV (but only through the window from outside the house).

5   They know how much I hate water but they still _____ me have a bath once a week.

3 TV

Read each definition and write the correct word at the end of each sentence.

> contestant   celebrity   ~~presenter~~   an episode
> serial   viewing figures   audience   viewers

1   the person who introduces a TV show
    _____*presenter*_____

2   statistics that show how many people watched a TV show _____

3   the people who watch a TV show being filmed in the studio _____

4   the people who watch TV at home _____

5   a TV show that tells a story over several weeks/ months _____

6   a famous person _____ .

7   one part of a TV show that runs for more than one week _____

8   someone who takes part in a TV quiz or game show

    _____

4 Anger

Complete with the words in the box.

> bit   bear   cool   ~~mad~~   cross
> headed   temper   tantrum

The day got off to a bad start and then just got worse. My sister was [1] *mad* with me because I spent too long in the bathroom. Then my dad [2] _____ my head off just because I started reading the paper before him. Honestly, he's so hot- [3] _____ . At least my other sister didn't shout at me. But then she hasn't said anything to me for about a week now. How can anyone [4] _____ a grudge for so long? As I was leaving the house my baby brother started having a [5] _____ . I left that one for my mum to sort out. School wasn't much better. My 'best' friend Lucy lost her [6] _____ with me just because I told Brian Curtis she likes him. I didn't know it was a secret. I told her to keep her [7] _____ but that just made things worse. Then finally Mr Pendleton got really [8] _____ at me because apparently I was talking in his lesson. I was only telling Brian that Lucy likes him.

1 Sport with a difference

1 Grammar

✷ Relative clauses: review

a Complete the text about the singer Madonna with the correct relative pronouns.

Madonna is a singer, composer and actor [1] _____who_____ was born in Bay City, Michigan in 1958. In 1977, she moved to New York [2] _____ she hoped to start her singing career. After a few months in New York she met a DJ, [3] _____ contacts in Warner Brothers gave Madonna the opportunity she was hoping for. *Holiday*, [4] _____ was one of her first songs, became an international hit. She starred as Eva Perón in the film *Evita*, a role [5] _____ won her many awards. She is not afraid to sing songs [6] _____ are controversial. Madonna, [7] _____ personal life is always in the news, has two children, Lourdes and Rocco. In 2001 she moved with her family to England, [8] _____ she now lives. In 2005 her album, *Confessions on a Dance Floor*, went straight to number one in forty different countries, breaking a record [9] _____ , until then, had only ever been held by The Beatles.

b Cross out the relative pronoun where it is unnecessary.

1 The concert ~~that~~ I wanted to go to had already sold out.
2 Those students who have passed their exams don't need to come to the revision course.
3 The man who Tony was speaking to is my boss.
4 Saturday, which is my birthday, is also my day off.
5 The pasta that I had for lunch was delicious.
6 The sauce that came with the pasta was amazing.
7 I got an email from the lady who I contacted about the youth hostel.
8 I have to take a train that stops in Birmingham.
9 The restaurant where we ate was very expensive.
10 The book that I'm reading is about the human mind.

c (Circle) the correct relative pronouns.

1 It's the first time (that) / what we've met, isn't it?
2 The girl who / whose place you're sitting in is coming back in a minute.
3 The place that / where I live is too quiet for me.
4 Everyone which / who replies will get a free CD.
5 What's the name of the film that / who won the Oscar?
6 I did a computer course what / which was really helpful.
7 The girl which / whose dog ran away is in my class.
8 Did you understand that / what he was saying?

d Tick (✔) the sentence, a or b, which has a similar meaning to the first statement in **bold**.

1 **Not all the children got flu.**
   a The children who went to the party got flu. ✔
   b The children, who went to the party, got flu. ☐
2 **They were looking for a restaurant with a smoking area.**
   a They went into the first restaurant which had a smoking area. ☐
   b They went into the first restaurant, which had a smoking area. ☐
3 **I wanted to go to Florence.**
   a I booked the first holiday I found which was in Florence. ☐
   b I booked the first holiday I found, which was in Florence. ☐
4 **No one was allowed into the room.**
   a The people who were late weren't allowed into the room. ☐
   b The people, who were late, weren't allowed into the room. ☐

e Join the two sentences to make one sentence using relative pronouns.

1 He's doing a course. The course lasts for three months.

He's doing a course that lasts for three months.

2 Kate won the tennis match. She played against Akeela.

---

3 I spoke to the man. The man works at the information desk.

---

4 Yesterday I met Jenny. Jenny's sister was in my class in college.

---

5 They've started training for the match. The match will decide the championship.

---

6 Suren has moved to London. He lived next door for three years.

---

7 I asked him to post the letter. I had written the letter to my cousin.

---

8 My brother booked a holiday to New York. He lived in New York for six months.

---

f Read the sentences. Some are correct and some have a word which should not be there. If a sentence is correct, put a tick (✔) in the space at the end of the line. If a word should not be there, cross it out and write the word in the space.

1 The girl who opened the door was her sister. ✔

2 The person whose his car is blocking yours is over there. _____

3 The place where I used to live that was called Newtown. _____

4 There were some good new bands at the concert that what I went to. _____

5 The bus that goes into town leaves from the corner. _____

6 The company that it makes these products is based in France. _____

7 My sister used to go out with a guy who drove a Ferrari. _____

8 The guesthouse where we stayed it had a lovely view. _____

2 Grammar

✱ Relative clauses with *which*

Match the two parts of the sentences.

1 You don't know what you're going to be asked on the day of the exam,

2 Some scientists say men and women are becoming more alike,

3 He moved to Edinburgh last year,

4 I need to buy a new car,

a which means I'll have to start saving.

b which means that opportunities could become more equal.

c which means we hardly get to see him.

d which makes preparation very difficult.

3 Vocabulary

✱ Sports

a Complete the crossword.

Across

4 Where you play tennis.

6 What you do to the ball with your foot in football.

8 Glasses you wear when you are swimming.

9 You need one of these to hit the ball in tennis.

Down

1 The name for the 'ball' in ice hockey.

2 For this sport, your board is no good if there aren't any waves.

3 Another name for a football field.

5 You wear these when it's cold or if you're a boxer.

7 This protects your head in aggressive or dangerous sports.

9 Where you go to ice-skate or to play ice hockey.

b (Circle) the correct words to complete the dialogue.

Paul: Who ¹*beat* / (won) the match on Saturday?

Rob: Rovers. They ²*beat* / *scored* United by two goals to one.

Paul: Who ³*drew* / *scored*?

Rob: Paul Smith ⁴*scored* / *won* the first goal. United got a goal back and it looked like they were going to ⁵*draw* / *win* in the end.

Paul: Then what happened?

Rob: Five minutes before the end, one of the United defenders was ⁶*beaten* / *sent off* and Rovers got a penalty, which Smith ⁷*beat* / *scored*. But if that player hadn't been sent off, I don't think United would have ⁸*beat* / *lost*.

4 Pronunciation

✱ Intonation in questions

a Look at the questions. Do you think the voice goes up ↑ or down ↓ at the end of each one of them?

1 What time does the flight take off?
   In about half an hour.

2 Are you going away for the weekend?
   No, I'm staying at home.

3 Do you want to go for a drive in my new car?
   I'd love to.

4 Where do we get off the bus for the museum?
   It's the next stop.

5 Will you send me a postcard when you get there?
   Of course I will.

6 Are you leaving for Paris tonight?
   Yes, at about ten thirty.

b ▶ **CD4 T2** Listen and check.

c ▶ **CD4 T2** Listen again and repeat the questions.

⑤ Culture in mind

a This is part of a web page about an Irish sport called 'hurling'. Read the text and match the words with the definitions.

1 sliotar
2 hurley
3 shinty
4 camogie

a the name of the stick used in the game
b a similar sport mostly played in Scotland
c a similar sport played by women
d the name of the ball used in the game

---

http://www.sportpedia.net/hurling

Sportpedia   definitions   top searches   news   discussions

Hurling

Hurling is an outdoor team sport of ancient Gaelic origin, and is played with sticks called *hurleys* and a ball called a *sliotar*. The game, played primarily in Ireland, has prehistoric origins and is thought to be the world's fastest field team sport. One of Ireland's native games, it shares a number of features with Gaelic football, such as the field and goals, number of players, and a lot of terminology. There is a similar game for women called *camogie*. It shares a common root with the sport of *shinty*, which is played predominantly in Scotland.

Hurling is played on a pitch 137–145 m long and 80–90 m wide. The goals at each end of the field are formed by two posts, which are usually 6 m high, set 6.4 m apart, and connected 2.44 m above the ground by a crossbar. A net extending at the back of the goal is attached to the crossbar and lower goalposts.

Teams consist of fifteen players, and five substitutions are allowed per game.

The object of the game is for players to use the *hurley* to hit the *sliotar* between the opponents' goalposts:

either over the crossbar for one point, or under the crossbar into a net guarded by a goalkeeper for a goal, which gets three points. The *sliotar* can be caught in the hand and carried for not more than four steps, struck in the air, or struck on the ground with the *hurley*. It can be kicked or slapped with an open hand (the hand pass) for short-range passing, but it cannot be thrown. A player who wants to carry the *sliotar* for more than three steps has to bounce or balance it on the end of the stick and it can only be handled twice while it's in his possession.

Side-to-side shouldering is allowed, but hitting someone with your body is illegal. No protective padding is worn by players. A plastic helmet with faceguard became obligatory for all age groups, including senior level, in January 2010.

Hurling is played throughout the world, and is especially popular where there are Irish communities, for example in the United Kingdom, North America, Europe, Australia, New Zealand, South Africa and Argentina.

---

b Read the text again. Mark the sentences *T* (true) or *F* (false).

1 Hurling is a slow sport.   *F*
2 There are two ways of scoring points in hurling. ☐
3 Players are allowed to use their hands as well as the *hurley*. ☐
4 Hurling players are not allowed to touch players of the other team. ☐
5 All hurling players have to wear a helmet. ☐
6 Hurling is played outside Ireland. ☐

c Read the text again and answer the questions.

1 What does the text tell us about the number of players?
2 In what way(s) is hurling similar to Gaelic football?
3 How can a player score three points in hurling?
4 How can a hurling player pass the ball (*sliotar*) to another player?
5 What is the main reason why hurling is popular in countries other than Ireland?

6 Listen

a Look at the pictures. What are the sports? Write down any words you know associated with these sports.

A _____

_____

B _____

_____

C _____

_____

D _____

_____

E _____

_____

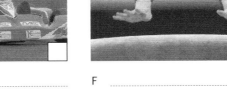

F _____

_____

b ▶ **CD4 T3** Listen to five short sports commentaries. Match the correct sport with each speaker. Write 1–5 in the boxes. There is one photo you won't use.

c Now write the words you heard that helped you choose each answer.

1 _____

2 _____

3 _____

4 _____

5 _____

EXAM TIP

Matching opinions with pictures

In this type of task you hear five short extracts which have a common theme.

- Before you start listening, look at all the information you have already.

- Think of everything you know about the subject and try to predict the words the speaker will use.

- Try to choose the answers during the first listening and check them during the second one.

- Some of the vocabulary can be difficult. Don't worry if you don't understand every word; just try to understand the general meaning.

Unit check

1 Fill in the spaces

Complete the text with the words in the box.

> which   whose   who   it   where   why   ~~who~~   what   when   that

Sabrina Cohen, [1] ___who___ is one of Wales's top martial arts fighters, has fought 101 rounds to raise money for cancer charities. 22-year-old Cohen, [2] _____ father died of cancer [3] _____ she was nine years old, fought the marathon in Cardiff, [4] _____ she lives. She had planned to fight 100 rounds, but in the end she did an extra one, [5] _____ she dedicated to her father's memory. 'This is for the man [6] _____ inspired me to do this,' she said. It is thought to be the first time [7] _____ such an event has been staged in the sport. 'It doesn't matter [8] _____ you do,' she said. 'The important thing is to make the effort. I'd definitely do [9] _____ again.' Her friends commented: 'We were concerned about Sabrina but we understood [10] _____ she wanted to do this and supported her all the way.' | 9 |

2 Choose the correct answers

(Circle) the correct answer: a, b or c.

1   The man ____ I met is from Chile.
    a which   b whose   c (who)

2   She didn't pass the exam, ____ means she has to repeat the year.
    a which   b what   c that

3   The person ____ lent me that film wants it back.
    a which   b whose   c that

4   The book ____ you ordered has arrived.
    a that   b it   c what

5   I don't understand ____ he's saying.
    a which   b that   c what

6   They couldn't give us the information ____ we needed.
    a it   b that   c what

7   ____ they need is a new director.
    a Who   b That   c What

8   The pitch ____ we played the match on was in really poor condition.
    a who   b that   c what

9   The boy ____ dog bit you apologised.
    a whose   b who   c which | 8 |

3 Vocabulary

Underline the correct words.

1   One of the two boxers fell out of the ring / court.

2   He played really well, and he scored / won the last goal too.

3   Make sure you wear your gloves / helmet – you don't want to hurt your head.

4   It was an exciting match. In the end, we drew / beat 2–2.

5   The referee sent him out / off in the tenth minute.

6   I'm sure that we're going to win / beat the next team we play.

7   I wanted to go swimming, but I forgot to take my racket / goggles, so I couldn't.

8   The pitch / rink we played on was in bad condition. It had almost no grass on it at all.

9   There are sixteen teams in our local football league / match. | 8 |

How did you do?

Total: | 25 |

Very good
20 – 25

OK
14 – 19

Review Unit 1 again
0 – 13

2 People are people

1 Grammar
* what clauses

a ▶ CD4 T4 **Listen to the embarrassing stories A–D. Write the correct letter beside the quote that matches it.**

1 'What was really embarrassing was that it took a couple of days for the colour to wash off.' ☐

2 'What was even worse was that I had to sing it all over again.' ☐

3 'What annoyed me most was my dad's reaction! I'll never forgive him.' ☐

4 'What made me feel bad was that the teacher had a bump on his head for the next week.' ☐

b **There is an extra word in some of these sentences. Cross out the extra word or tick (✔) if the sentence is correct.**

1 This is what I like ~~that~~ best about the job. ....

2 What annoys me is about Josie is that she's always talking. ....

3 What you see is what you get. ....

4 What I need to concentrate on that is grammar. ....

5 I like what thing she says about the course. ....

6 It doesn't matter what you say, she never listens. ....

c **Join the two sentences to make one sentence using what.**

1 Anne is always late. It annoys me.

   What annoys me about Anne is that she is always late.

2 John always changes his mind. It's very frustrating.

   ....

3 She argues a lot with her sister. It makes life difficult for her parents.

   ....

4 The teachers ask you to do things. It's essential to do them.

   ....

5 That restaurant has a good atmosphere. This makes it special.

   ....

6 You should do certain things when people are hurt. It's good to know them.

   ....

2 Pronunciation
* Sentence stress and rhythm

a ▶ CD4 T5 **Listen and underline the stressed words.**

1 What I really want to do is have a rest.
2 I never listen to what he says.
3 What really impressed me was her presentation.
4 I never know what to say in these situations.
5 What I would like to know is where we are all going to stay.
6 This isn't what you were saying last week.

b ▶ CD4 T5 **Listen again and repeat.**

3 Vocabulary
* Personality adjectives

a **Match the descriptions 1–6 with the adjectives a–f.**

1 someone who is caring and understanding
2 someone who is superficial
3 someone who is silly and forgetful
4 someone who is clever and funny
5 someone who is very pleased
6 someone who is happy and full of energy

a bubbly
b smug
c shallow
d sympathetic
e witty
f scatty

b Which person do the quotes refer to? Write the numbers 1–4 in the boxes.

a Sorry, no eating in class!

b Oops!

c Katie, you look great! What's your secret?

d My father always says that what counts is who you know...

1 Ralph is so pretentious. He's always talking about famous people that he's met and pretending he's important.

2 He's so hypocritical!

3 Carl is so careless. He never looks where he's going!

4 I love meeting up with Mike. He's so charming. He always makes me feel good.

c Complete the sentences with the words in the box.

> pushy ~~intellectual~~ shallow
> cheeky smug sympathetic

1 Walter loves learning and thinking. He's really _intellectual_ .

2 Don't be _____ . It's not nice to answer back to people.

3 Be careful. She's very _____ . She'll try to get you to do what she wants.

4 Rachel's very _____ these days. She must have been given a promotion.

5 The teacher was very _____ when she heard my bag had been stolen.

6 Don't expect her to understand if you've got a problem. She's quite _____ .

d **Vocabulary bank** Complete the crossword.

			²E	³C	C	E	N	T	R	I	⁴C	

(crossword grid with numbered cells 1–10)

Across

2 James is so __eccentric__ ! He does the craziest things.

5 Don't be _____ ! Let other people have a go.

9 She seems a bit pushy, but in fact she's very _____ when you get to know her.

10 He lent me his bike and walked home! What an _____ thing to do.

Down

1 She doesn't seem very happy about getting promoted. She's pretty _____ about her promotion.

3 She never gets too excited – she's a very _____ person.

4 You drank all the milk and there's nothing left for us! That's not very _____ , is it?

6 He's always jumping up and down and laughing – he's a very _____ person.

7 Don't look so sad – you need to be a bit more _____ about things.

8 He never understands anything, because he's not very _____ .

4 Grammar

✳ Verbs + gerund/infinitive review

a (Circle) the correct words to complete the horoscopes.

this month's horoscope ...

Aquarius
You'll enjoy *to be* / (being) the centre of attention today.

Pisces
Try not *to repeat* / *repeating* the same mistakes over and over again.

Aries
You can't stand *to follow* / *following* the crowd. Today is no exception.

Taurus
Have you borrowed any money from anyone recently? Remember *to pay* / *paying* them back today or you could get into trouble.

Gemini
Don't stop *to believe* / *believing* in yourself and you'll get what you want.

Cancer
Don't refuse *to meet* / *meeting* a friend today. They could be important for your future.

Leo
Don't stop *to talk* / *talking* to a stranger you'll meet today. They'll waste your time.

Virgo
Can you remember ever *to feel* / *feeling* so happy? Make the most of this special time!

Libra
It's time you stopped *to think* / *thinking* about the past. You need to live in the present.

Scorpio
You enjoy *to be* / *being* outdoors. Take time off work and go for a walk.

Sagittarius
Take time to stop *to think* / *thinking* about what's going on around you. You might miss something important if you don't.

Capricorn
Try not *to lose* / *losing* your temper with a friend or someone in your family. You'll be glad you made the effort.

b Complete the dialogue with the correct form of the verbs in brackets.

Dave: What took you so long?

Jane: I stopped [1] *to buy* (buy) some food on the way.

Dave: Oh good! Did you remember [2] _____ (get) some milk?

Jane: Yes! Guess who I met at the supermarket ... Sally Watson!

Dave: Sally Watson? I remember [3] _____ (be) friends with her. In fact, we used to go out with each other when we were about eighteen.

Jane: Really? Why did you stop [4] _____ (go out) with her?

Dave: We were just different. I enjoyed [5] _____ (go) to parties and [6] _____ (meet) people. She couldn't stand [7] _____ (hang around) with my friends. I haven't heard from her for ages.

Jane: Well, she was asking about you. She gave me her new phone number.

Dave: Really?

Jane: Yeah, here it is. Don't forget [8] _____ (call) her! It sounds like she wants to meet up again.

5 Everyday English

a Complete each expression with one word.

1 I can _____live_____ without ...

2 Mind _____ .

3 _____ chance!

4 I'd _____ thought ...

5 ... and _____ on.

6 Don't look _____ me.

b Complete the dialogues with the expressions from Exercise 5a.

1 A: Hey – someone's eaten all the chocolate!

   B: Well, _____ . I don't even like chocolate very much.

2 A: Do you think we'll win the match on Sunday?

   B: _____ ! They're a much, much better team than us.

3 A: What kind of books does he like?

   B: Oh, you know – thrillers, detective stories, police novels _____ .

4 A: Hey – _____ . You're in my way.

   B: Oh, sorry. I didn't know you were trying to get past.

5 A: Let me give you some advice.

   B: No, _____ it, thanks. The last time I took your advice, things got worse!

6 A: Do you think I can ask Mr Bryant about my problem?

   B: Well, yes, _____ so. He's usually very approachable.

6 Study help

✳ Using a range of vocabulary when writing

- One way of improving your writing skills is to avoid repeating yourself by using an appropriate range of vocabulary. This is particularly important when writing a story or an essay.

- Before you start writing, think of key words that you will use, then write down synonyms for them. You can also write adjectives or nouns that you associate with the key words.

- When you have finished, re-read your text and find an alternative for repeated words or phrases. You can use the words from your list. Use a dictionary to check the exact meaning of the synonyms.

Match the underlined words with their meanings a–d.

1 Poi is the hottest pastime of the year among British teenagers. Everyone is doing it.

2 The Harry Potter craze has made reading very popular with young people and helped bookshops greatly increase their sales.

3 Last year's fashion fad, wearing coloured braces on your teeth, has passed. What's going to replace it?

4 When something is in fashion, it's popular and lots of people want to buy or have it.

a a passing trend or one that lasts for a short time

b a trend that is followed with great enthusiasm

c the current trend

d latest and most exciting

Skills in mind

7 Write a story

a Read these two texts. Do they contain the same information?

Text 1

He opened the door. The room was dark and untidy. He turned on the light. The room was bigger than it seemed. There were books everywhere. Bookshelves were on the walls and there were books on the table and on the chairs. Books covered the floor.

John panicked. He would never find the book he was looking for.

b Read the two texts again and answer the questions.

1 What is the difference between the texts?
2 What does the descriptive language in Text 2 tell us about John?
3 What does the descriptive language in Text 2 tell us about the room?
4 Do you think that John has been in the room before?
5 Why do you think he is looking for his mother's diary?

c Now continue the story.

Then, suddenly, he saw it on the table beside his mother's favourite chair. Of course... He was shaking as he walked over and picked it up, holding his breath as he turned to the first entry.

Text 2

Slowly he turned the key in the door. His hand was shaking, but, carefully, he pushed the door open. The heavy curtains were drawn and it was dark and gloomy inside.

It was obvious, even in the half-light, that no one had been in here for a long time. He stepped in and almost fell over a mountain of books on the floor. The room was in a complete mess. There were books everywhere. Old books were packed into the bookshelves that lined the walls of the room. Every surface was covered with books and papers. Dictionaries and reference books were lying all over the centre table. He took one of these books from the table and turned towards an armchair. It was also covered with books of every sort: atlases, novels, and dictionaries in languages he didn't recognise.

Everywhere he looked there were books. Where had they all come from? And where was the cosy library that he used to go in as a young boy? Where had it disappeared to?

John felt his heart fill with fear and panic. How was he going to find his mother's diary amongst all these books? Would he never find out the truth about what happened that night?

Unit check

1 Fill in the spaces

Complete the text with the words in the box.

| being   pretentious   secret   loved   excitement   to be   ~~shy~~   witty   whenever   tried to |

The English novelist Jane Austen was born in 1775. She was ¹ _____shy_____ as a child and didn't enjoy
² _____ in the spotlight. Austen's life was quite boring and without great ³ _____ or
change. She was educated at home by her father, and ⁴ _____ reading and writing. She didn't want
⁵ _____ noticed, so she kept her writing a ⁶ _____ and wrote on small pieces of paper
which she hid ⁷ _____ anyone came into the room. Her father supported her and
⁸ _____ find a publisher for her. Her novels are famous for making fun of anyone who is smug
or selfish. In her writing, she is very critical of ⁹ _____ people, and her heroines are always
intelligent as well as ¹⁰ _____ and attractive.

9

2 Choose the correct answers

Circle the correct answer: a, b or c.

1 I _____ my boyfriend at a party.
   a knew   b (met)   c made
2 Karl has got a terrible _____ of humour.
   a sensitive   b mood   c sense
3 Did you enjoy _____ to her?
   a talk   b talking   c to talk
4 Sally refused _____ at the conference.
   a speak   b speaking   c to speak
5 Don't go near Stuart. He's in a really bad _____ .
   a mood   b nature   c sense

6 I've _____ her since I was at primary school.
   a found   b met   c known
7 Tell Anne about your problem. She's
   very _____ .
   a sympathetic   b smug   c scatty
8 I can't stand _____ this any longer.
   a do   b doing   c to do
9 Please, try _____ . There was nothing else
   I could do.
   a understand   b to understand
   c understanding

8

3 Vocabulary

Underline the correct words.

1 Someone who is clever and creative is _bright_ / cheeky / scatty.
2 Someone who listens and cares is smug / careless / sympathetic.
3 Someone who doesn't get too excited is excitable / calm / bubbly.
4 Someone who always tries to get what they want is pushy / shallow / cheeky.
5 Someone who takes a positive view of things is downbeat / upbeat / careless.
6 Someone who does unusual things is unapproachable / pretentious / eccentric.
7 Someone who forgets things easily is scatty / pushy / witty.
8 Someone who you can go and talk to is unselfish / approachable / upbeat.
9 Someone who talks back to people is shallow / cheeky / selfish.

8

How did you do?

Total: 25

  Very good 20 – 25   OK 14 – 19    Review Unit 2 again 0 – 13

3 Time travellers

1 Grammar

✷ Reported speech

a Match the two parts of the sentences in each group.

1 Caroline told Sara
2 Sara said,
3 Marco told

a Sara that Caroline was making a mistake.
b that she was going to move to Canada.
c 'I'm going to miss you.'

4 John said
5 The teacher told
6 I told him

d that Russian was quite difficult.
e to me that he wanted to study Russian next year.
f him he would have to learn the Russian alphabet before he started.

7 My dad told
8 He said
9 I told

g him that I was scared of horses.
h me he wanted to take me horse riding at the weekend.
i he had booked us a lesson at 11 o'clock on Saturday.

b (Circle) the correct words in the second sentence.

1 She told me that she couldn't come to the meeting.
'I (can't) / couldn't come to the meeting.'

2 He told me to call him if I needed help.
'You call / Call me if you need help.'

3 The teacher asked her if she had taken the letter to the head teacher.
'Did you take / Would you take this letter to the head teacher?'

4 He said he would call to see her the following day.
'I'd call / I'll call to see you tomorrow.'

5 Steven said he had seen Mark the previous day.
'I've seen / I saw Mark yesterday.'

6 He told me that he was going out with Susana that evening.
'I go out / I'm going out with Susana this evening.'

c Rewrite these sentences using direct speech.

1 He asked me if I had seen *Harry Potter and the Deathly Hallows*.
Have you seen Harry Potter and the Deathly Hallows?

2 I replied that I hadn't but that I was reading the book.

3 He asked me if I would lend him the book when I had finished with it.

4 I asked him what he knew about the author.

5 He told me that the author, J. K. Rowling, had always wanted to write books.

2 Vocabulary

✱ Expressions with *time*

a Look at the cartoon and read the joke. Tick (✔) the funniest answer 1, 2 or 3.

Q: What time was it when the elephant sat on the clock?

A: _____

1 I don't know. ☐

2 Two o'clock? ☐

3 Time to get a new clock! ☐

b Complete the sentences with the correct tense of the verbs in the box.

> give   spend   take   waste

1 There was no deadline on the project, so we _____ our time.

2 I hate visiting my brother. He always _____ me a hard time about my job.

3 He's really fit. He _____ most of his free time at the gym.

4 'So far this evening, you _____ a lot of time watching TV. Do some homework!'

c (Circle) the correct preposition.

1 I'm taking some time *off / on* work to redecorate the house.

2 I phoned just *at / in* time to get the last tickets.

3 The new teacher never arrives *at / on* time.

4 We didn't get the painting finished properly because we ran *off / out* of time.

d Complete the sentences with the word in **bold** at the end. You will need to use more than one word.

1 Don't ___*waste time*___ during the exam. (**waste**)

2 He's taking some _____ because he's been working hard recently. (**off**)

3 You can _____ , the train doesn't leave until six. (**take**)

4 I don't think I passed the test. I _____ and I didn't answer all the questions. (**ran**)

5 She arrived _____ to hear him. (**just**)

e 🔲 **Vocabulary bank** Complete the sentences with the words in the box.

> to kill   to lose   a matter of
> of all   a lot of   ~~of my life~~   from

1 I had the time ___*of my life*___ in Paris.

2 Who do you think is the best rock singer _____ time?

3 My mother travels to the USA _____ time to time.

4 Hurry up! There's no time _____ !

5 One day we'll win the championship, I'm sure. It's just _____ time.

6 I like Jean. I've got _____ time for her.

7 The play doesn't start for another two hours, so we've got a lot of time _____ .

3 Pronunciation

✱ The schwa /ə/

a 🔲 **CD4 T6** Listen to the sentences. <u>Underline</u> the unstressed syllables. They all contain the schwa /ə/ sound.

1 Teach<u>ers</u> don't of<u>ten</u> have <u>a</u> lot <u>of</u> time.

2 He wastes a lot of time on the Internet.

3 Michael arrived just in time to have dinner with us.

4 You can take some time off next week when we're not so busy.

5 Have you got time for a cup of tea?

b 🔲 **CD4 T6** Listen again and repeat.

4 Grammar

✳ Reporting verbs

a Match the two parts of the sentences. Write the letters a–h in the boxes.

1 Cathy reminded her father   `g`
2 In the letter he had persuaded   ☐
3 She said that   ☐
4 And she advised   ☐
5 She recommended   ☐
6 The book encourages   ☐
7 It also suggests   ☐
8 Cathy asked her dad to promise   ☐

a her to stay at school.
b she was worried about him.
c over-worked and stressed people to relax.
d a book to him.
e to think about her advice.
f that they learn to do things more slowly.
g about a letter he had written to her when she was fifteen.
h him to stop working so hard.

b ▶ **CD4 T7** Cathy rings her father. Listen and ⟨circle⟩ the correct words to complete the statements.

1 Cathy rings her father and asks if he has ⟨received⟩ / *sent* her letter.
2 He says that he *got* / *sent* it the week before.
3 He says he *didn't read it* / *didn't read it properly.*
4 Cathy tells him to *take time off* / *work hard.*
5 At first, her father *refuses* / *wants* to listen to her.
6 He promises to *read the letter* / *take time off* once they have finished the phone call.

c Rewrite the sentences so they have the same meaning. Use the verbs in **bold** at the end.

1 'I'll be on time tomorrow morning!' (**promise**)
He promised that he would be on time the next morning.

2 'You should buy the latest Coldplay album.' (**recommend**)
Laura _____ .

3 'Don't ever do that again!' (**warn**)
Their mum _____ .

4 'Let's go to the cinema at the weekend.' (**suggest**)
She _____ .

5 'I wouldn't buy that mobile phone.' (**advise**)
Jane _____ .

6 'If you join our gym you'll be super fit in just a month.' (**claim**)
The instructor _____ .

7 'I didn't break the vase.' (**deny**)
She _____ .

8 'And I won't accept homework that isn't done on time.' (**emphasise**)
The teacher _____ .

5 Literature in mind

a Read this extract from H. G. Wells's *The Time Machine*. (Circle) the word a, b or c that is closest in meaning to the words numbered 1–8 in the text.

The time traveller is thousands of years in the future. He has stopped the machine to look at the world around him.

The machine was standing on a sloping beach. The sea stretched away to the south-west, rising into a sharp bright horizon against the ¹wan sky.

There were no waves, because there wasn't a breath of wind. Only a slight oily swell rose and fell like a gentle breathing, and showed that the sea was still moving and alive. And along the water's edge was a thick layer of salt, that was pink under the ²lurid sky. There was a sense of oppression in my head, and I noticed that I was breathing very fast. The sensation reminded me of my only experience of mountaineering, and from that I realised that the air was ³more rarefied than it is in our times.

Far away, up the desolate slope, I heard a ⁴harsh scream, and saw something like a huge white butterfly go flying up into the sky and then, circling, it disappeared over some low ⁵hillocks in the distance. The sound of its voice was so ⁶dismal that I shivered and sat more firmly on the machine. Looking round me again, I saw that, quite near, what I had thought was a reddish piece of rock was moving slowly towards me. Then I saw that it was really a monstrous crab-like creature. Can you imagine a crab as large as a table, with its legs moving slowly and uncertainly, its big claws ⁷swaying, its long antennae, like whips, waving and feeling, and its eyes ⁸gleaming at you on either side of its metallic front? I could see the feelers in its mouth moving around as it came towards me.

1 a wet   b (pale)   c closed
2 a curious   b delicious   c brightly-coloured
3 a thinner   b more delicious   c lower
4 a black   b funny   c unpleasantly strong
5 a small birds   b small rivers   c small hills
6 a very sad   b very happy   c very quiet
7 a walking very quickly   b moving from side to side
   c shouting loudly
8 a shining brightly   b laughing   c closing

b Read the text again and answer the questions.

1 How did the traveller know that the sea was still alive?

2 How did the traveller know that the air in the future was thinner?

3 Why did the traveller sit 'more firmly on the machine'?

4 What did the traveller think the crab-like creature was, at first?

6 Read

a Read this extract from *The Hitchhiker's Guide to the Galaxy* by Douglas Adams. Is it about the past, the present or the future?
Give reasons for your answer.

It is an important and popular fact that things are not always what they seem. For instance, on the planet Earth, man had always assumed that he was more intelligent than dolphins because he had achieved so much – the wheel, New York, wars and so on – whilst all the dolphins had ever done was muck about in the water having a good time. But [1] conversely, the dolphins had always believed they were far more intelligent than man – for precisely the same reasons.

Curiously enough, the dolphins had long known of the impending destruction of the planet Earth, and had made many attempts to alert mankind to the danger; but most of their communications were misinterpreted as amusing attempts to punch footballs or whistle for [2] titbits, so they eventually gave up and left the Earth shortly before the Vogons arrived.

The last ever dolphin message was misinterpreted as a surprisingly [3] sophisticated attempt to do a double-backwards somersault through a hoop whilst whistling The Star-Spangled Banner, but in fact the message was this: So long, and thanks for all the fish.

In fact there was only one species on the planet more intelligent than dolphins, and they spent a lot of time in research laboratories running around inside wheels and conducting frighteningly [4] elegant and [5] subtle experiments on man. The fact that once again man completely [6] misinterpreted this relationship was entirely according to these creatures' plans.

b Match the words in the text 1–6 with the definitions a–f.

a small pieces of food *titbits*
b on the other hand
c understood something different
d clever and complicated
e graceful and attractive
f clever but not obvious

c Choose the correct answer: a, b or c.

1 Why did man think he was more intelligent than dolphins?

  a Because man didn't understand dolphins.

  b Because man thought he had achieved more than dolphins.

  c Because New York was an important city.

2 What does 'muck about' mean?

  a Swim.   b Perform tricks.   c Play.

3 What did the dolphins know that man didn't?

  a That the planet Earth was going to be destroyed.

  b That *The Star-Spangled Banner* had a secret meaning.

  c That the Vogons liked fish.

4 What was 'entirely according to these creatures' plans'?

  a That they spent a long time in labs.

  b That man did not understand what they were really doing.

  c That they were more intelligent than dolphins.

EXAM TIP

Multiple choice

- Always skim through the text to get a general idea of its meaning.

- Read the questions carefully before reading the text again.

- If you are unsure, eliminate any obviously incorrect answers first. When you choose an answer, try to find a logical reason for your choice.

Unit check

1 Fill in the spaces

Complete the text with the words in the box.

| has promised | time | that | asked | on | spent | ~~last~~ | warned | denied | offering |

This is a report from [1] _____last_____ Friday's Student Council meeting. Everyone arrived [2] _____ time. The chairperson, Pete, [3] _____ everyone to give their opinion on the quality of the food in the school canteen. Caroline said [4] _____ she thought the meals were quite good. She also suggested [5] _____ more vegetarian and organic meals. Karl [6] _____ that organic food in particular would be more expensive. Jonathan said they had [7] _____ enough time talking about organic food during the last meeting. Pete asked Jonathan not to waste [8] _____ arguing with the others and Jonathan left. Some people claimed that insects had been found in some meals recently but a representative from the canteen [9] _____ this. Pete wrote a report and the head teacher [10] _____ to read it as soon as possible.

| | 9 |

2 Choose the correct answers

Circle the correct answer: a, b or c.

1 Catherine asked us _____ our opinions on the play.
   a give   b (to give)   c giving

2 She denied _____ about the letter.
   a knowing   b to know   c know

3 He convinced her _____ it.
   a doing   b to do   c do

4 The teacher warned us _____ it.
   a not doing   b not to do   c to don't

5 He said that he _____ I would be happy.
   a hopes   b is hoping   c hoped

6 She _____ Angela all about her holiday.
   a said   b told   c told to

7 She promised _____ the next time she was in the area.
   a calling   b that she call   c to call

8 I decided _____ anything about the misunderstanding.
   a not saying   b not to say   c not that I say

9 He told _____ that he had tickets for the concert.
   a to me   b I   c me

| | 8 |

3 Vocabulary

Complete the sentences. Write one word in each space.

1 I _____spend_____ a lot of time every day on the internet.

2 That's a really ridiculous question. Please don't _____ my time.

3 He was really tired, so he took some time _____ work and went on holiday.

4 I think Rafael Nadal is the best tennis player of _____ time.

5 The party was fantastic!! I had the time of my _____ .

6 If I get home late, my parents always _____ me a hard time.

7 Hurry up! We're running _____ of time!

8 We were nearly late, but we got there just _____ time to catch the bus.

9 There's no hurry. We can _____ our time.

| | 8 |

How did you do?

Total: | 25 |

| :) | Very good 20 – 25 | :| | OK 14 – 19 | :(| Review Unit 3 again 0 – 13 |

4 In and out of fashion

1 Grammar

※ used to and would

a Tick (✔) the sentences if you can replace *used to* with *would*.

1 During the holidays we used to play outside until it was dark. ✔

2 My dad used to whistle while he was working. ☐

3 The dog used to follow her everywhere. ☐

4 They used to arrive at the end of June and stay until September. ☐

5 She used to have green hair. ☐

6 I used to have a horse but I sold it. ☐

b Complete the table with information about what we do now.

	then	now
1	sent telegrams	*send emails*
2	used candles	
3	made their own toys	
4	travelled in carriages	
5	wrote letters	
6	wore long skirts and dresses	
7	listened to records	
8	had lots of children	

c Write sentences using the information in the table.

1 *In the past, people used to send telegrams, now they send emails.*

2 _____

3 _____

4 _____

5 _____

6 _____

7 _____

8 _____

d Complete the sentences with the verbs in the box. Use *would* where you can or *used to*.

> spend ~~want~~ drive
> be   not go   find

1 I *used to want* to be a teacher but now I think I'll be a doctor.

2 They _____ hours playing cards every evening.

3 I _____ languages quite difficult, but now I speak Italian and Russian fluently.

4 You're a successful businesswoman now. It's hard to believe you _____ a punk.

5 When I was a kid I _____ anywhere without my teddy.

6 He _____ a Ford. Now he's got a BMW.

2 Vocabulary

✱ In and out of fashion

Complete the article with the words in the box.

> catch on   hooked   overwhelming
> launched   craze   spread

Shoppers looking for a natural high were able to satisfy their needs by inhaling, or breathing in, flavoured oxygen from the first oxygen bar to be [1] _launched_ in Cardiff. Inhaling oxygen through a tube is a new [2] _____ which is expected to [3] _____ in nightclubs across the UK. The trend started in Tokyo, but it has quickly [4] _____ to Britain and the US. 'The demand has been [5] _____,' says the manager of the bar, Neil Lucas.

Some customers say they are already [6] _____ on the experience. 'You feel really good and full of energy afterwards,' says Ray, a local businessman.

3 Vocabulary

✱ Adverbial phrases

a Join the two sentences to make one, using adverbial phrases. There is sometimes more than one possibility.

1 He looked at me. He seemed surprised.

   He looked at me with surprise.

2 The dog barked at us. It sounded horrible.

   _____

3 He teaches English. His way of teaching is fun.

   _____

4 They listened to her. They were enthusiastic.

   _____

5 We found the house. It was difficult to find.

   _____

6 He said hello to me. He was friendly.

   _____

7 We need to do this again. We need to do something different.

   _____

8 The children waited for the clown to arrive. They were excited.

   _____

b (Circle) the correct adverbial phrase to complete the sentences.

You might be told it's wrong to look at people [1] (*in a rude way*)/ *in a surprising way*, but a new craze called Stare Master is winning fans across America. People are queuing up [2] *with difficulty / with enthusiasm* to take part in staring contests. The Stare Master contests are held [3] *in public / on purpose* and have really strict rules – you aren't allowed to laugh, close your eyes, nod or move. 'It's great,' said one fan, 'because it tests your self-control [4] *in a different way / in a horrible way.*' It was invented by two friends because they were bored and wanted to spend their free time in [5] *a fun way / a friendly way.*

4 Grammar

✱ Comparing adverbs

Make sentences comparing the actions. Use the adverbs and *as ... as.*

1 Mary (eats / drinks / quickly)

   Mary eats as quickly as she drinks.

2 He (reads / talks / slowly)

   _____

   _____

3 Frank (doesn't work / plays / hard)

   _____

   _____

4 She (plays the guitar / sings / nicely)

   _____

   _____

5 We (arrived / could / soon)

   _____

   _____

6 I (don't speak French / speak Spanish / well)

   _____

   _____

5 Vocabulary

✳ Common adverbial phrases

a (Circle) the correct adverbial phrase.

1 She's the first person to be voted chairperson three years *in public* / (*in a row*).

2 They held the meeting *on purpose* / *in private* and no one knew anything about it.

3 Can you call a taxi for me? I'm *in a hurry* / *in a row* to get to the station.

4 Please don't tell anyone, I was told *on purpose* / *in secret*.

5 Can you help Janet? She's *in a panic* / *in a hurry* about the exam.

6 I don't like talking *in public* / *in private*. Crowds make me nervous.

7 I think he said it *by accident* / *on purpose* to make everyone laugh.

8 Don't be angry. She did it *by accident* / *on purpose*. It's not like her to cause problems.

b Complete the puzzle. Use the mystery word to complete the last sentence.

1 When you do things in front of other people, you do them in _____ .

2 When you have to do something quickly you're in a _____ .

3 When you don't want everyone to see what you're doing, you do it in _____ .

4 If you worry and get anxious about something, you are in a ____*panic*____ .

5 If you do the same thing lots of times, you do it several times in a _____ .

6 If you hide something from other people, you do it in _____ .

7 If you don't mean to do something, you do it by _____ .

8 When you do something on _____ , you mean to do it.

c **Vocabulary bank** Complete the sentences with the words in the box.

back	out	down	~~bottom~~	wrong	toe

1 The house was really dirty, so we cleaned it from top to ____*bottom*____ .

2 Your pullover looks kind of strange – I think it's inside _____ .

3 Sorry, that's not right – the words are the _____ way round.

4 You've got your T-shirt on _____ to front.

5 He was covered in mud from head to _____ .

6 Turn the bottle upside _____ and shake it – then the sauce will come out.

6 Pronunciation

✳ /æ/ *sat* and /e/ *set*

a ▶ **CD4 T8** Listen and (circle) the correct word.

1 He lost his (*bat*) / *bet*.

2 Have you got my *pan* / *pen*?

3 It's *Dad* / *dead*!

4 There's a *band* / *bend* in the road.

5 The cat *sat* / *set* by the fire.

6 The *man* / *men* can stay.

b ▶ **CD4 T8** Listen again and repeat.

7 Read

a Read the text. Complete the sentences with one word in each space. There is often more than one possibility.

Fashion & music

We're used to seeing music stars like Madonna and Lady Gaga wear fashions which [1] _create_ an image for them. But music and fashion have always been closely linked. The tough, leather-wearing image of early rock stars [2] _____ Gene Vincent influenced a generation of young people in Europe and in the USA. A cultural war [3] _____ out in the mid-1960s in the UK over the rivalry between the 'Mods' (who favoured high-fashion, expensive styles) and the 'Rockers' (who wore T-shirts and leather); followers of each style had their favourite musical acts, who fed into the rivalry by releasing records praising one style and criticising the other. In the 1960s, The Beatles brought mop-top haircuts, collarless blazers and Beatle Boots into fashion.

Rock musicians were among the first people to wear hippie fashion, and introduced such styles as the Nehru jacket; bands like The Beatles wore custom-made clothes that had a strong [4] _____ on 1960s style. As rock music genres developed, what an artist wore became as [5] _____ as the music itself in defining the artist's intent and relationship to the audience. The glam rock of the 1970s brought fashion to new [6] _____ of importance in rock music with the 'glitter' image of artists like T. Rex. Some artists who had been active in the late 1960s, such as David Bowie, also adopted a glam-influenced look.

In the late 1970s, disco acts helped make flashy urban styles fashionable, while new wave groups started wearing mock-conservative [7] _____ including suit jackets and thin ties, in an [8] _____ to be as different from mainstream rockers as possible.

In the early 1990s, the popularity of grunge brought in a fashion of its own. Grunge musicians and fans wore torn jeans, old shoes, flannel shirts and backwards baseball hats, and grew their hair against the clean-cut image that was popular at the [9] _____, together with a heavily commercialised pop music culture. Musicians continue to be fashion icons; pop-culture magazines such as *Rolling Stone* often [10] _____ fashion sections featuring musicians as models.

b ▶ CD4 T9 Listen to the radio phone-in. Four people talk about their favourite 'songs about fashion'. Complete the chart with the names in the box.

> *Vogue*   The Kinks   George Michael   *Freedom*   David Bowie
> *Dedicated Follower of Fashion*   Madonna   *Fashion*

Speaker	Song name	Artist
Speaker 1: Janine		
Speaker 2: Andy		
Speaker 3: Phyllis		
Speaker 4: Mark		

8 Listen

a ▶ **CD4 T10** Listen to the radio presenter introduce Philippa Chandler. Make notes about who she is and what she does.

b Answer *T* (true), *F* (false) or *D* (doesn't say) below.

1 Philippa Chandler is a radio presenter. ☐
2 *The People Show* features fashionable people. ☐
3 Next Big Thing is a company that predicts new trends. ☐

c ▶ **CD4 T10** Before you listen again, (circle) the best answer, a, b or c, to complete the sentences below. Then listen to check.

1 Philippa's job is to
   a write about new trends.
   b start new trends.
   c help her clients create new trends.

2 A regular part of Philippa's work is to
   a join clubs.
   b go to popular surf resorts.
   c carry out surveys.

3 Philippa found out about her current job
   a thanks to a newspaper article.
   b from a friend.
   c through a freelance job agency.

4 Philippa believed she was perfect for the job because
   a she loved clubbing and surfing the net.
   b she is sociable and had done research on why we buy things.
   c she is curious and likes asking people questions.

d Answer the questions. You may need to listen again.

1 Explain, in your own words, what is meant by the 'next big thing'?

2 Why are Philippa's clients interested in the information she collects?

3 When is Philippa's research not productive?

4 What advice does Philippa give young people looking for a job?

EXAM TIP

Question types in listening

● Before you start, read the questions thoroughly and make sure you understand them. Underline key words and try to predict what you will hear.

● There may be different types of question. In Exercise 8, there are three question types.

   Type 1 You decide if the statement is true or false or if you don't have enough information to answer it.

   Type 2 You decide which answer completes the phrase best. Remember in this type, you may hear all the phrases given, but only one is relevant to the question.

   Type 3 You answer the questions, usually with a short or complete sentence. Always check your spelling, grammar and punctuation.

Unit check

1 Fill in the spaces

Complete the text with the words in the box.

| popular fashion are concerned ~~hottest~~ potentially demand for a start warnings sharing group |

Bebo is one of the [1] _hottest_ websites among young people. It's aimed at people aged 13–30 but it's most [2] _____ with students. Bebo allows you to chat with your friends, [3] _____ space on the web together. 'There is a huge [4] _____ for this type of service,' says Bebo's boss, Michael Birch. When you join Bebo you choose a school or college and join its [5] _____ of members. Some teachers [6] _____ about the service and have stopped their students using it during school hours. [7] _____ , students are wasting study time. But, more importantly, the site is [8] _____ dangerous because students can share personal details. Students might think this [9] _____ is just a bit of fun but things can go wrong if they give information to the wrong person,' says one worried head teacher, who wants the site to have more [10] _____ about the risks. [9]

2 Choose the correct answers

Circle the correct answer: a, b or c.

1 I _____ have long hair.
   a would   b (used to)   c was used to

2 He smiled at me in a _____ way.
   a friendly   b friends   c friendliness

3 Rachel sang as nicely _____ she did the last time I heard her.
   a than   b more   c as

4 I _____ have a dog when I was a child but I haven't got any pets now.
   a would   b should   c used to

5 I answered all the questions, but _____ .
   a difficult way   b with difficulty   c with difficult

6 They're completely hooked _____ that new TV series.
   a on   b to   c up

7 The craze caught _____ immediately.
   a up   b in   c on

8 The fashion _____ swept through schools in Britain.
   a quick   b in a quickly way   c quickly

9 Fans reacted _____ when they discovered that the tickets were sold out.
   a angrily   b with angrily   c angry   [8]

3 Vocabulary

Complete each sentence with one word.

1 I had an accident because I was _in_ a hurry.

2 It was a total surprise. He'd done everything _____ secret.

3 I didn't think he would want to come, but he accepted _____ great enthusiasm.

4 I deleted some files on my computer _____ accident – I was so angry with myself!

5 Can I talk to you _____ private for a few minutes?

6 Monday, Tuesday and now Wednesday – you've been late three days in a _____ .

7 I put my shorts on back to _____ .

8 The CD-ROM didn't play because I'd put it _____ down in the computer.

9 I don't think it was an accident – I'm sure he did it on _____ !   [8]

How did you do?

Total: [25]

| :) Very good 20 – 25 | :\| OK 14 – 19 | :(Review Unit 4 again 0 – 13 |

5 Do something!

1 Grammar

✳ Conditionals review

a Match the two parts of the sentences. Write the letters a–h in the boxes.

1 If you want to get involved with a charity, `d`   a she'll get a really bad headache.
2 If you wanted to be useful in some way, ☐   b we'll raise lots of money for the charity.
3 If she walks too fast at this altitude, ☐   c he wouldn't have played.
4 If she'd walked any faster at this altitude, ☐   d there are lots of things you can do.
5 If we get lots of sponsors, ☐   e he won't play.
6 If we had more sponsors, ☐   f there'd be lots of things you could do.
7 If he's feeling ill, ☐   g she'd have got a really bad headache.
8 If he'd been feeling ill, ☐   h we'd raise lots of money for the charity.

b Match the sentences with the pictures. Write 1–6 in the boxes.

1 It won't be difficult if you get fit.
2 If they'd played better, they'd have won.
3 You'd enjoy yourself more if you danced.
4 If you were fit, it wouldn't be difficult.
5 If they play better than last week, they'll win.
6 You'd have enjoyed yourself more if you'd danced.

c Complete the sentences with the correct form of the verbs in brackets.

1 If we'd found more sponsors, we _would have raised_ (raise) more money for the charity.
2 I'd be a volunteer if I _____ (have) more time.
3 If Jackie _____ (go) on the sponsored walk next week, I'll go with her.
4 If I could go anywhere in the world, I _____ (visit) the Himalayas.
5 I think I'd freeze to death if I _____ (not have) my sleeping bag in the tent.
6 If I _____ (not go) on the Himalayas trip, I'll regret it for the rest of my life.
7 If anyone makes a racist comment during tomorrow's match, we _____ (throw) them out of the stadium.
8 We'd have won the match if the coach _____ (make) us train harder.

2 Vocabulary

✱ Ways of getting involved

a Complete the puzzle.

1 We're trying to raise *money* for sick children.
2 Our charity needs money, so please make a ________ .
3 I don't get paid for this – this is ________ work.
4 We went to the town centre to hand out ________ .
5 We're going to make a ________ against the new law.
6 Charities need lots of people to ________ them out.
7 Don't just sit around and do nothing – get ________ !
8 We need lots of people to sign our ________ .
9 Eddie Izzard ran 43 ________ .

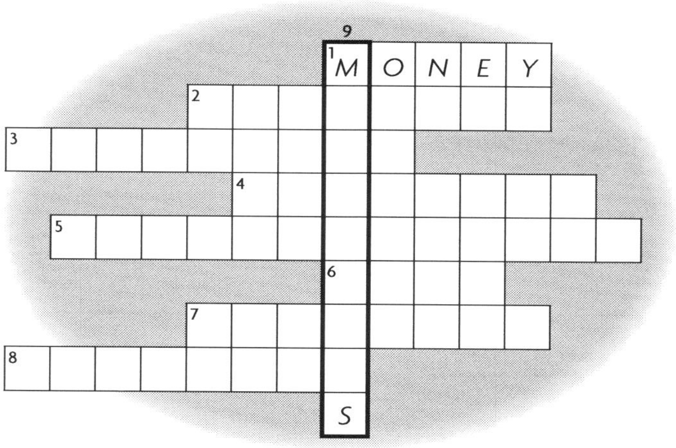

b Complete the text with the correct form of the words from the crossword.

At our school, there's a big mixture of kids from different cultures, so for our charity work this year we decided to [1] *raise* money for Show Racism the Red Card – it's an organisation that works against racism in football. We decided to [2] ________ out by organising a football match between two teams, both of which had black and white players in them, and we raised almost £1,000. Some other kids gave up their free time to do [3] ________ work like going into the town centre to hand out [4] ________ . These explained why racism is a bad thing, and asked people to make [5] ________ to the organisation. Then the next weekend, lots of us went to a football match and we made a [6] ________ outside the stadium before the match started. We also got lots of people to sign our [7] ________ against racism – we got over 500 signatures! So it was a great experience, and we all learned that it's brilliant to get [8] ________ in this kind of thing.

c **Vocabulary bank** Complete the sentences with words in the box.

backed	collaborated	~~worker~~	aid
voluntary	volunteered	with	hand

1 My brother's gone to be an aid *worker* in Central America.
2 Everyone at school ________ me when I entered the charity run.
3 If you have any problems, phone me and I'll come and give you a ________ .
4 After the earthquake, hundreds of people ________ to help find survivors.
5 John and I ________ on this project – see, both our names are there.
6 They're collecting money in ________ of cancer research.
7 I only managed to do this ________ the aid of my family and friends.
8 She does ________ work for a charity two afternoons a week.

3 Pronunciation

✱ Contractions in third conditionals

▶ CD4 T11 Listen and repeat. How do you pronounce the underlined sounds?

1 If you'd eaten that, you'd have been ill.
2 If you'd asked me, I'd have told you.
3 If you hadn't told him, he wouldn't have known!
4 I'd have been delighted if you'd come.
5 It would have been difficult if he'd been there.
6 Would you have come if we'd invited you?

4 Grammar
✻ Mixed conditionals

a Read the sentences. If a sentence refers to the *past only*, write 'PO' at the end. If a sentence refers to the *past and present*, write 'PP' at the end.

1 If we'd stayed in a different hotel, our holiday would have been better. *PO*

2 I wouldn't have had such a good time if you hadn't come with me. ....

3 If I hadn't played in the match yesterday, I wouldn't be so tired today. ....

4 I'd have taken more photos if I'd had more time. ....

5 I'd be happier if the exam had been a bit easier. ....

6 I'd have gone on the sponsored walk if I wasn't so busy. ....

b Match the pictures with the sentences. Write 1–6 in the boxes. There are three sentences you won't need.

1 If I hadn't gone on holiday, I'd be able to buy a motorbike.

2 If I'd gone on holiday, I wouldn't be able to buy a motorbike.

3 If I had a good memory, I'd have passed.

4 If I didn't have a good memory, I wouldn't have passed.

5 If I didn't speak Japanese, I wouldn't have understood.

6 If I spoke Japanese, I would have understood.

c Match the two parts of the sentences.

1 If it wasn't a great DVD, *c*

2 If it was a great DVD, ☐

3 If he was a good student, ☐

4 If he wasn't a good student, ☐

5 The party would be better ☐

6 The party wouldn't be so good ☐

7 If she liked you, ☐

8 If she didn't like you, ☐

a if I'd remembered to bring my CDs along.

b she would have phoned you.

c I wouldn't have bought it.

d he wouldn't have failed the exams.

e I would have bought it.

f if I hadn't remembered to bring my CDs along.

g she wouldn't have phoned you.

h he would have failed the exams.

d Join the two sentences with a mixed conditional.

1 She doesn't speak Spanish. She didn't understand.
If she spoke Spanish, she would have understood.

2 I don't swim well. I didn't win the race.

....

....

3 She has worked extremely hard. She's successful.

....

....

4 My brother loves U2. He spent €200 on a ticket for their concert.

....

....

5 I hate action films. I didn't go to see *Iron Man 2*.

....

....

5 Culture in mind

a Read the text and (circle) the correct answer: a, b, or c.

For which charity / charities does The Bogle Stroll raise money?

a   Cancer Research

b   AIDS research

c   The text doesn't say.

'The Bogle Stroll'

History

Back in 1961, a group of teachers from the University of Manchester missed the last bus and were walking home at night from Lancaster to Manchester, a distance of almost 90 kilometres, when they thought they saw a 'bogle' (a kind of ghost). They decided to create a charity walk called 'The Bogle Stroll'. It has run every year since then and is now one of the longest-running sponsored events in the country.

The Events

Although The Bogle is famous for being a sponsored walk, it also offers participants the option of cycling the event. Currently comprising four main events, the Bogle features several distances that range in difficulty.

The Bogle Stroll is the most popular event of the four, where participants walk just under 90 kilometres through the night around Manchester. Participants walk what are called the North and South Loops, which form a figure of eight around Manchester. Every year, only about 50% of those who enter the event finish.

The Bogle Ramble is a shorter alternative to the Bogle Stroll, covering approximately 40 kilometres around the north of Manchester. Participants don't walk through the night. They just walk the North Bogle Loop, finishing back at the start point.

The Bogle Wander is the shortest of the four events: participants walk approximately 20 kilometres of the North Bogle Loop. The Bogle Wander may be the shortest route, but it's still not an easy challenge.

The Bogle Roll is an alternative event, which gives participants the chance to cycle the route rather than walk. Cyclists cover approximately 125 kilometres by riding the North Bogle Loop three times whilst tackling various hills and difficult stretches of road.

Event Organisation

The event is run entirely by full-time students in Manchester. It also relies on a large team of volunteers who are responsible for the overall safety and management of checkpoints located along the route.

Money raised

In 2010, The Bogle Stroll raised around £17,000 for charity.

b Read the text again. Answer the questions.

1   Why is the event called 'The <u>Bogle</u> Stroll'?

2   Which of these shapes shows the basic route of the Stroll?

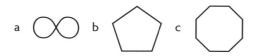

3   How many people usually complete the event?

4   What are the two main differences between The Stroll and The Ramble?

5   In what way is The Bogle Roll different from all the other events?

6   Who gets involved in running the event?

6 Read

a Greenpeace is an international environmental organisation. Complete their webpage with the phrases in the box.

> let your imagination run wild   informs or inspires you
> who want to get involved   saved ancient forests from logging
> speak with one voice   will make all the difference

GREENPEACE International

Make a donation

We don't accept donations from governments or corporations, so the money we need to do our work comes from people like you. Your donation
1 _____ .

Become a Cyberactivist

Our global community of Greenpeace people comes from 125 countries. We have a long list of successes to prove that when people
2 _____ ,
they can change the world. Sign up and you'll get our e-zine, a monthly electronic magazine, which is full of ways you can help. It's all free. Sign up!

Visit our Action Forum

Take part in the online community that has changed climate-damaging policies, stopped the killing of hundreds of whales in Iceland,
3 _____ ,
and had many other successes. You'll get a free homepage, and a chance to meet other people
4 _____ .

Spread the word!

Any time you see something on the Greenpeace site that interests,
5 _____ ,
send it to a friend. Write letters to the editor of your local paper. Buy a Greenpeace T-shirt and wear it!

GET INVOLVED

Green computer users

Are you into computers? You can help us spread the word by creating something for us. A screensaver, perhaps? A game about the environment?
6 _____ !!

Send us your ideas at supporter. services@int.greenpeace.org, and if it's cool and it works, we'll use it and send you a gift to say thank you.

b Read the text again. Mark each sentence *T* (true) or *F* (false).

1 Greenpeace gets money from governments. [F]

2 If you join Greenpeace, you'll get a free electronic magazine every week. [ ]

3 Greenpeace has prevented whales in Iceland from being killed. [ ]

4 Greenpeace suggests that you write letters to the editor of their newspaper. [ ]

5 Greenpeace wants people to send all kinds of information technology ideas. [ ]

6 Greenpeace will pay you if they use your ideas. [ ]

EXAM TIP

True / false exercises

- Read the statements carefully, so that you know what each one really means.

- Find the relevant part of the text for each statement.

- Watch out for expressions which are similar in meaning, for example *get money* and *receive donations*.

- There will be a mixture of true and false statements.

Unit check

1 Fill in the spaces

Complete the text with the words in the box.

> I finished   volunteers   sponsored
> I'd be   handed   support   involved
> I'd finished   donation   ~~raise~~

A few weeks ago, I read about a 20 km run to ¹ ___raise___ money for a little girl who needs an operation to save her life, so I decided to get ² _____ . At first, I thought about making a ³ _____ , but then I read that they wanted ⁴ _____ to join the run. I thought: 'If I needed an operation, ⁵ _____ really happy if people tried to help me.' So I decided to join the run. A lot of people ⁶ _____ me – if ⁷ _____ the run, I'd get £100 for the charity. On the day of the run, my family and friends came to ⁸ _____ me. The organisers ⁹ _____ out numbers to all the runners. After about 12 km, I had to stop so I didn't get any money from the sponsors. I was furious with myself – if ¹⁰ _____ the run, that little girl would have £100 more for her operation. I sent a cheque to the charity anyway.

`9`

2 Choose the correct answers

Circle the correct answer: a, b or c.

1 We're trying to _____ £1,000 for charity.
   a (raise)   b rise   c rest

2 Would you like to _____ a donation?
   a do   b make   c pay

3 We're going into town to _____ out leaflets.
   a hand   b look   c take

4 On Saturday I'm going on a big _____ against experiments on animals.
   a petition   b manifestation   c demonstration

5 We need people to _____ our work.
   a support   b involve   c sign

6 If you'd worn a coat, you _____ cold now.
   a wouldn't be   b hadn't been   c weren't

7 The charity has paid employees, but it also needs _____ to help out.
   a frees   b involvers   c volunteers

8 I'd have less trouble with these questions if they _____ easier.
   a will be   b would be   c were

9 If I was a climber, I _____ to the top of the mountain.
   a had gone   b would have gone   c went

`8`

3 Vocabulary

Underline the correct words.

1 Would you like to make a _donation_ / money / support to our charity?
2 We're collecting money in help / aid / save of homeless people.
3 Our job will be a lot easier if we support / demonstrate / collaborate with each other.
4 This is really heavy – can you give me a help / hand / aid?
5 I did a charity run and I raised / won / handed out more than £150 for charity.
6 Nobody forced him to go into the army – he's a supporter / volunteer / donation.
7 It's their problem, not mine. I don't want to get volunteer / organised / involved.
8 There's going to be a big demonstration / marathon / petition against racism in London next weekend.
9 Would you like to hand out / sign / join this petition?

`8`

How did you do?

Total: `25`

| 😄 | Very good 20 – 25 | 😐 | OK 14 – 19 | 😞 | Review Unit 5 again 0 – 13 |

6 Our world

1 Grammar

✳ Future continuous

a Here is Sara's diary page for tomorrow. Write a sentence about what she will be doing at each of the times.

1 At 8.30 tomorrow *she'll be flying to Paris.*

2 At 10.45 tomorrow _____ .

3 At 13.00 _____ .

4 At 16.00 _____ .

5 At 17.30 _____ .

6 At 19.00 _____ .

7 At 21.30 _____ .

8 At midnight _____ .

b Write sentences about the year 2030.

1 People / live / houses under the sea
People will be living in houses under the sea.

2 We / not eat / any natural food

_____

_____

3 Children / study / at home on computers

_____

_____

4 We / drive / electric cars

_____

_____

5 We / not use / telephones

_____

_____

6 People / not work / more than 25 hours a week

_____

_____

15th August

08.00 – 08.55	Fly to Paris
10.00 – 11.30	Discuss the new Paris shop with George
12.00 – 13.30	Have lunch with Alain Dupont
14.00 – 17.00	Interview people for the shop manager's job
17.00 – 18.00	Visit the Le Clerc factory
18.15 – 19.30	Look at the new designs
21.10 – 21.55	Fly back to Manchester
23.00 – 00.30	Watch the film on TV!

2 Grammar

✳ Future perfect

a Complete the sentences with the future perfect form of the verbs in brackets.

1 I _will have finished_ (finish) my homework by 10 o'clock.

2 I think they _____ (find) a cure for cancer by 2015.

3 By 2090, the world's population _____ (increase) to about 30 billion.

4 Please don't phone me at 3.00 – I _____ (not leave) school by then.

5 Next year, my parents _____ (be) married for 25 years.

6 How _____ (our lives / change) by the year 2050?

7 Go and buy a ticket before midday, otherwise they _____ (sell) them all.

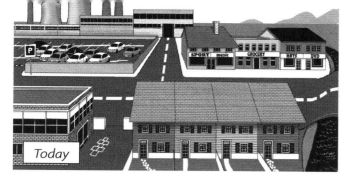

Today

PARKING

AIRPORT

SUPERMARKET

20 years' time

b Use the words to write sentences about the future of the town in the pictures.

1 They / build / airport
They will have built an airport.

2 The school / disappear

3 The river / dry up

4 The shops / become / supermarket

5 They / close down / factory

6 They / put / car park underground

7 People / put / solar panels / the roofs of their houses

c (Circle) the correct tense: future continuous or future perfect.

1 Don't phone me at 8 tonight – we'll (be having) / *have had* dinner then.

2 When I'm 25, we'll *be living / have lived* in the USA for five years.

3 At 11 o'clock tomorrow morning, I *will have done / will be doing* an examination.

4 By the end of the weekend, my brother *will have played / will be playing* five football matches!

5 If you want to see the game, call this afternoon, when we *will be watching / will have watched* it.

6 Next Wednesday morning, we *will be sitting / will have sat* on the beach in Greece!

3 Pronunciation

✱ /ð/ *the* and /θ/ *thing*

a ▶ **CD4 T12** Listen and put the words in the correct place.

~~other~~	bath	month	brother
clothes	thin	weather	
Thursday	thirsty	theatre	

/θ/ *thing*	/ð/ *the*
	other

b ▶ **CD4 T13** Listen and repeat.

1 I think their brother is thin.

2 There are three rooms with a bath.

3 I thought I saw them at the theatre last month.

4 My mother bought new clothes on Thursday.

4 Vocabulary

✱ Global issues

a Complete the text with the words in the box.

starvation	species	atmosphere
waste	temperature	~~resources~~

Making the future **brighter**?

Many of the world's natural [1] *resources* are running out and the [2] _____ of the sea is going up, increasing the chances of polar ice melting. Global warming is also increasing due to pollution in the [3] _____ , mainly because of the use of fossil fuels like coal and oil. We could use more nuclear energy – but what do we do with the [4] _____ ? And then there is the fact that many [5] _____ of animal are becoming extinct, and members of our own human race are dying through [6] _____ and war. What can we do? Well, let's look at some ideas…

b Replace the words in *italics* with the correct form of the verbs in the box.

~~bring about~~ die out use up get rid of foul up go up

1 Support organisations which are trying to ~~cause~~ *bring about* an end to trade in rare animals.

2 Don't buy medicines and other products which result in animals *becoming extinct* _____.

3 Remember that every time you travel by car or plane, you cause the temperature of the air *to increase* _____.

4 Let's stop *polluting* _____ our air, water and land.

5 You don't need all those electrical machines – *dispose of* _____ some of them!

6 Remember that if we go on using oil and coal the way we do, they will be *completely finished* _____ in a few years' time.

5 Study help

✳ Learning phrasal verbs

● **The meanings of phrasal verbs**
You should make a note of new phrasal verbs in a vocabulary notebook, including the new item in a sentence which clearly shows its meaning.

My sister and I made up five minutes after we argued.

Other methods you can use include synonyms. However, you must remember that these words will not always be directly interchangeable. It's also a good idea to make a note of some of the common collocations you'll find with the phrasal verb.

make up with someone

You should also note any other meanings. *Make up* can also mean to invent a story, e.g. *My father made up lots of stories to tell me when I was little.*

Check the register (degree of formality). Phrasal verbs are often (but not always) quite colloquial and more commonly used in spoken language.

Finally you might like to use translation.

● **Grouping phrasal verbs**
Some students like to use grouping to help them learn 'sets' of new phrasal verbs.

– grouping by verb (e.g. *stand by someone / stand up for something / stand in for someone*, etc.)

– grouping by preposition (e.g. *turn on / bring on / get on*, etc.)

– grouping by topic (e.g. journeys – *a plane takes off / set off on an adventure / get back from holiday*, etc.)

Circle the correct phrasal verbs to complete the text.

OUR GLOBAL VILLAGE

Wherever you are these days, you will [1] *come across* / *meet up with* products that are available globally, even if you are a long way from home. Fast food restaurants [2] *take up* / *turn up* in smaller towns as well as cities, you are never far from a can of Coca–Cola or Pepsi, and there is always a Hollywood film at a cinema near you to [3] *sit out* / *sit back* and enjoy. Supporters of globalisation say it gives developing countries a chance to [4] *bring round* / *turn into* richer, more powerful economies through tourism and trade. Why should people [5] *turn down* / *take back* the chance to have a better lifestyle? Others say that workers in developing countries continue to [6] *take on* / *put up* lower–paid jobs, even if they may now work for a global company. Can globalisation help to end poverty? Or does it just make the rich even richer? Whatever the answer, we should [7] *stand up for* / *put up with* people in poverty. We have to [8] *look into* / *look up* the ways that big, international companies work and try to make sure that they are as fair as possible for everyone.

6 Everyday English

a Complete the expressions with the words in the box.

~~ever~~   break   face   mind   hang   business

1   what_ever_

2   Are you out of your _____ ?

3   _____ on a minute!

4   Give me a _____ !

5   It's none of your _____ .

6   Let's _____ it...

b Complete the dialogue with the expressions in Exercise 6a.

Nick: Hey, Mike, do you want to go out tonight?

Mike: I can't. I've got to get up tomorrow at four in the morning.

Nick: 4 o'clock. [1] _____ ? Why on earth would anyone want to get up at that time?

Mike: Well, [2] _____ actually.

Nick: Oh, go on. Tell me.

Mike: OK. But I don't want any of your usual comments.

Nick: I promise I won't say anything.

Mike: We're going on an anti-global warming demonstration in London and I've got to catch the early coach.

Nick: Anti-global warming? [3] _____ . You don't really believe in that nonsense, do you?

Mike: You promised you wouldn't say anything.

Nick: I know but it's all such rubbish. I mean even if it was true, you're not going to change anything by going on a silly demonstration. [4] _____ , Mike – you're just wasting your time.

Mike: [5] _____ , Nick. I'm not really that interested in what you think and I've got to get going anyway.

Nick: So who else is going on this demonstration?

Mike: Just me, Tom and his girlfriend Julia and Debbie Hands.

Nick: Debbie Hands? Oh. Is it too late to get a coach ticket?

Mike: [6] _____ . You've just been telling me what a waste of time it all is and now you suddenly want to come along?

Nick: Yes, but you didn't say anything about Debbie Hands before.

7 Study help

✳ Noticing language

• When you read texts in English or listen to people speaking English, you will mainly be trying to understand the message. But it can be very useful to notice not only *what* people say or write, but also *how* they say or write it.

• You probably know that there are some areas of English that you are unsure about. This could be to do with tenses (for example, the present perfect) or with words (for example, the difference between *until* and *by*).

• Make a note of any areas you feel unsure about. Then, when you are reading something, see if the text has any examples of this. If it does, stop and read again. Which words or verb tense did the person use to express their meaning? Try to remember these examples.

• You will remember these things better when you have noticed enough examples. You will notice more if you read and listen to as much English as you can.

8 Write

a Read this letter quickly and answer the questions.

1 What is the person writing about?
2 What does he hope will happen?

b Read the letter again. Mark the statements *T* (true) or *F* (false).

1 The writer says he is completely against the proposal for a new supermarket. ☐

2 He thinks it's important to look at the positive and negative sides of the question. ☐

3 He does not believe that the supermarket will bring jobs for young people. ☐

4 The writer will find shopping more convenient if there is a supermarket. ☐

5 There are lorries in the roads of Whitefields estate at night. ☐

6 The writer hopes that the local authority will listen to what people think. ☐

c Imagine a large change to the area where you live. This could be:

an airport
a new road
new buildings (factories / shops / supermarkets)
an idea of your own

Write a letter to a newspaper. Describe the planned change and its possible effects, and how you feel about them.

WRITING TIP

Rhetorical questions

- A rhetorical question is a question that we ask without really expecting an answer from anyone – it is a question asked to make an impact on the listener or reader.

- Find and underline three rhetorical questions that Tom asks in his letter. For each one, decide what he wanted to ask.

Readers' thoughts

Dear Sir,

There is a plan to build a new supermarket on the edge of the Whitefields housing estate, on the land where the local library now is. I live at Whitefields, and I would like to express my concern about this plan. It is not that I am completely against the idea of building a supermarket – I just think that as a community we need to weigh up the advantages and disadvantages before committing ourselves.

It is clear that the library is underused and in poor condition. It is also clear that there are very few shops near here and a supermarket would be a good thing to have. But the people who want to build the supermarket seem to think that no one wants the library any more, that it isn't needed because of the internet and so on. Is this necessarily true, especially for elderly people? What about young people who don't have the internet at home and need to go to the library to do their homework? Where can they study if they have to share a room with a younger brother or sister?

On the other hand, there is an argument that a new supermarket would not only bring more choice of shopping and more convenience for local residents, but it would also bring some much-needed jobs for younger people in the town – and this is a good point.

What we need to do is consider the effect a supermarket will have on our quality of life. Certainly the residents of the housing estate (including me) will find shopping a lot easier and more convenient. But there will also be extra traffic. In a few years from now, the roads in and around the estate will be full of cars in the daytime and delivery lorries at night, and not only that – we will have got used to it, too. Are more jobs and more convenience worth such an impact on our daily lives? Perhaps, but this is what we have to ask ourselves.

I believe that all the residents of Whitefields, and the local authority, need to discuss this question in an open-minded way – and I hope that by the time a decision is taken, we will have had a full and fair discussion of the issues involved, and that the local authority will have really listened to everyone's views. Is that too much to ask?

Yours faithfully,
Tom Watkins (by email)

Unit check

1 Fill in the spaces

Complete the text with the words in the box.

> dying   will be   species   will have
> bring about   will need   starvation
> ~~resources~~   is going   have become

Animals are one of the most important ¹ _resources_ for human beings, especially farm animals. But in the past 100 years, over 1,000 breeds of animal ² _____ extinct. Still today, some ³ _____ of farm and domestic animals are ⁴ _____ out. This is a major problem, because the number of people in the world ⁵ _____ up – some scientists say that by 2050, the population ⁶ _____ doubled. This means that in 40 years' time we ⁷ _____ more food to feed the world. 'It's a serious problem,' said a UN representative. 'We probably have until 2020 to stop the process. If we don't, then we ⁸ _____ losing some species at the rate of two a week. We have to ⁹ _____ a change of attitude and make sure that farmers continue to use many different kinds of animal. If we don't, this will increase the risk of ¹⁰ _____ in the future.'

| 9 |

2 Choose the correct answers

(Circle) the correct answer: a, b or c.

1 By 2030, many species will have _____ .
   a used up   b (died out)   c gone up

2 If the world's _____ goes up any more, there won't be enough cold water in the sea.
   a temperature   b atmosphere   c pollution

3 Don't call me after nine. I will _____ .
   a leave   b have left   c be left

4 I need to _____ some old clothes.
   a foul up   b bring about   c get rid of

5 In 100 years we'll all _____ on another planet.
   a live   b be living   c have lived

6 We have the _____ to end hunger.
   a resources   b starvation   c species

7 If we go on like this, we're going to _____ all our planet's resources. There won't be any left.
   a die out   b recycle   c use up

8 This time next week, I will _____ on a beach in Spain. I can't wait.
   a sit   b be sitting   c have sat

9 The game will _____ by the time we get there!
   a have finished   b be finished   c finish

| 8 |

3 Vocabulary

Underline the correct words.

1 The black rhino is in danger of dying *up* / *out* / *over* in the next few years.
2 Why didn't you tell me you've used *out* / *under* / *up* all the printer ink?
3 Don't you think it's time you got rid *of* / *out* / *about* that teddy bear? You're 15!
4 The cars in most big cities are fouling *out* / *above* / *up* the air.
5 Buy the TV now. It's going *over* / *above* / *up* by £200 at the end of the week.
6 We need a prime minister who will bring *about* / *up* / *around* real change.
7 There are more than 10,000 *species* / *resources* / *makes* of birds in the world.
8 There's no reason why anyone in the modern world should die of *waste* / *temperature* / *starvation*.
9 They don't have the *waste* / *atmosphere* / *resources* to deal with such a huge natural disaster.

| 8 |

How did you do?

Total: | 25 |

 Very good 20 – 25   OK 14 – 19   Review Unit 6 again 0 – 13

7 Peacemakers

1 Grammar

✴ Past perfect passive

a (Circle) the correct tenses to complete the sentences.

1 I couldn't believe it – I *was* / (*had been*) chosen to play in the school football team.

2 I *was* / *had been* told off at school today for not paying attention.

3 The lottery winnings *were* / *had been* shared by ten people this week.

4 When they opened the door, they saw the painting *was* / *had been* stolen.

5 I was so angry when I found that my diary *was* / *had been* read by someone.

6 Everyone in the Olympic stadium stood up and clapped. The world record *was* / *had been* broken.

7 When she said 'no' all my dreams *were* / *had been* instantly destroyed.

b Tim wasn't in when his parents returned home early from their holiday. Look at the picture and use the words to make sentences.

1 vase / break

   A vase had been broken.

2 front window / leave open

   ....

3 sofa / tear

   ....

4 TV / leave on

   ....

5 books and CDs / not tidy away

   ....

6 letters / not collect

   ....

c Rewrite the sentences using the past perfect passive. Use the words in **bold** at the end.

1 When we got to the party, there wasn't any food left. (**eaten**)

   When we got to the party, all the food had been eaten.

2 I opened my bag and saw that my wallet wasn't there. (**stolen**)

   ....

3 The street was very different – there were no more trees there. (**cut down**)

   ....

4 When I got home, the TV was working again. (**fixed**)

   ....

5 I didn't go to the party because no one sent me an invitation. (**invited**)

   ....

6 We didn't watch the programme because we didn't know about it. (**told**)

   ....

2 Grammar

✱ Past perfect continuous

a In 2004, Wangari Maathai received the Nobel Peace Prize for her environmental work in Kenya. Read the text about her and her Green Belt Movement and complete the text with the words in the box.

> been causing   not studied   spent
> become known   been developing
> played   ~~always been~~   been fighting

Kenyan President Daniel Arap Moi and his government had ¹ _always been_ happy to help out big business even if this wasn't always best for the environment. At the same time, Wangari Maathai and her Green Belt Movement had ² _____ to save the land.

Ever since the organisation started in 1977, it had ³ _____ the Kenyan government problems. In 1989 the two sides met for their biggest showdown.

That year, the Green Belt Movement learned that powerful friends of the President had ⁴ _____ plans to build a 60-floor office building in the heart of Uhuru Park in the capital city Nairobi. The park had ⁵ _____ an important part in city life for many years, and it was the only place in Nairobi where families could go and enjoy the outdoors. When the Movement launched its campaign against the 'monster-park' as the building had ⁶ _____ , Wangari Maathai was often laughed at in public for not understanding development. Although she was the first to admit that she had ⁷ _____ town planning at university, she was smart enough to know that you need such spaces in large cities. Luckily, so were thousands of other Kenyans who joined the campaign and the park was saved. But the victory didn't finish there. The very same government who had ⁸ _____ so much time laughing at Maathai and her movement have now made Uhuru Park a national park.

b Use the verbs in **bold** and the past perfect simple (once) or the past perfect continuous (once) to complete each pair of sentences.

1 (walk)
  a We were hungry because we _had been walking_ all day.
  b When we got back to the hotel we _had walked_ 20 km.

2 (read)
  a By the end of the school holidays I _____ the three *Lord of the Rings* books.
  b I _____ for two hours so when I turned out the light I fell asleep immediately.

3 (save)
  a I started in March and by October I _____ enough money to buy a round-the-world air ticket.
  b I _____ for two years but I still didn't have enough money.

4 (eat)
  a We _____ all day and I couldn't eat any more.
  b When he arrived we _____ everything, so I made him a quick sandwich.

5 (watch)
  a He got a headache because he _____ TV all day.
  b By the end of the evening, we _____ all six *Star Wars* films.

6 (talk)
  a When I saw her yesterday she _____ to her teacher and she was feeling better.
  b She _____ on the phone for so long, she was really thirsty.

7 (cook)
  a He _____ all morning and there was a great smell from the kitchen.
  b He _____ me a birthday meal. I was so happy.

8 (write)
  a My hand was aching because I _____ since 10 o'clock.
  b I _____ the letter but was I brave enough to send it?

3 Vocabulary

✷ Conflicts and solutions

a Read the newspaper article and circle the correct answer: a, b, c or d.

Have you fallen ¹ _out_ with an old friend? Do you need to sort things ² _____ with a member of your family? Or do you want to make ³ _____ with your boyfriend or girlfriend?

If your answer to any of these questions is 'yes', then don't worry – help is at hand. *The Record* is proud to welcome one of the country's top agony aunts, Claire Hands, who will be writing exclusively for our paper as of next week. Claire has more than 20 years' experience of helping people ⁴ _____ compromises and ⁵ _____ conflicts. Claire knows that there are always two people to listen to and promises not to take ⁶ _____ .

By ⁷ _____ neutral, Claire is confident she can give you the advice you need to get your life back on track. So if you've got a problem and are ⁸ _____ , drop Claire a line today.

askclaire@therecord.co.uk

1 a up   b in   c (out)   d on
2 a out   b over   c with   d for
3 a in   b up   c on   d down
4 a get   b have   c look   d reach
5 a resolve   b finish   c break   d fix
6 a issues   b part   c sides
   d perspective
7 a waiting   b staying   c having
   d finding
8 a stuck   b broken   c missing
   d fixed

b [Vocabulary bank] Complete the dialogue with the words in the box.

> pick a fight   give-and-take   to the bottom
> on speaking terms   misunderstanding   negotiate
> ~~ill feeling~~   by the horns   come to blows   quarrel

Ana: Did I detect a bit of ¹ _ill feeling_ between you and Dan today?

Matt: Yes. We're not ² _____ .

Ana: Again! So what did you ³ _____ about this time?

Matt: I'm not sure really. I think he just wanted to ⁴ _____ with someone and I happened to be in the wrong place at the wrong time.

Ana: What! He hit you?

Matt: No, no. It didn't ⁵ _____ . He just started shouting at me for some reason.

Ana: There must have been some reason. Don't you want to get ⁶ _____ of it?

Matt: Well, there was a ⁷ _____ about his bike but I'm not sure exactly what.

Ana: Do you want me to say something to him for you?

Matt: What? Try and ⁸ _____ with Dan? You'll be wasting your time.

Ana: I don't understand you and Dan – best friends but always falling out. You know it's all about ⁹ _____ , don't you?

Matt: You should take the bull ¹⁰ _____ and tell that to Dan. Then maybe he wouldn't get so angry when I take his bike without asking.

4 Pronunciation

✷ Consonants at the end of words

a ▶ **CD4 T14** Listen and look at the underlined sounds. Tick (✔) the sentence in each pair where the hard consonant sound disappears.

1 a   Have they ma<u>de</u> up yet?   ☐
   b   She ma<u>de</u> Paul say sorry.   ☐

2 a   Let's try and <u>sort</u> out the problem.   ☐
   b   Let's try and <u>sort</u> the problem out.   ☐

3 a   Why do you always <u>take</u> sides?   ☐
   b   Can you <u>take</u> out the rubbish?   ☐

4 a   I always <u>get</u> stuck with my Maths homework.   ☐
   b   <u>Get</u> out of my room. I'm working.   ☐

b ▶ **CD4 T14** Listen again and repeat.

5 Literature in mind

Here is an extract from *Lord of the Flies* by William Golding. The leader, Ralph, is being chased by other boys.

He stumbled over a root and the cry that [1]pursued him rose even higher. [...] Then he was down, rolling over and over in the warm sand, crouching with arm up to ward off, trying to cry for mercy.

He staggered to his feet, tensed for more terrors, and looked up at a huge peaked cap. [...]

A naval officer stood on the sand, looking down at Ralph in wary astonishment. On the beach behind him was a [2]cutter, her bows hauled up and held by two ratings. In the stern-sheets another rating held a sub-machine gun. [...]

The officer looked at Ralph doubtfully for a moment, then took his hand away from the butt of the revolver.

'Hullo.'

Squirming a little, conscious of his filthy appearance, Ralph answered shyly.

'Hullo.'

The officer nodded, as if a question had been answered.

'Are there any adults – any grown-ups with you?'

[3]Dumbly, Ralph shook his head. He turned a half-pace on the sand. A semicircle of little boys, their bodies streaked with coloured clay, sharp sticks in their hands, were standing on the beach making no noise at all.

'Fun and games,' said the officer. [...]

The officer [4]grinned cheerfully at Ralph.

'We saw your smoke. What have you been doing? Having a war or something?'

Ralph nodded.

The officer inspected the little scarecrow in front of him. The kid needed a bath, a hair-cut, a nose-wipe and a good deal of ointment.

'Nobody killed, I hope? Any dead bodies?'

'Only two. And they're gone.'

The officer leaned down and looked closely at Ralph.

'Two? Killed?'

Ralph nodded again. Behind him, the whole island was shuddering with flames. The officer knew, [5]as a rule, when people were telling the truth. He whistled softly. [...]

'We'll take you off. How many of you are there?'

Ralph shook his head. The officer looked past him to the group of painted boys.

'Who's boss here?'

'I am,' said Ralph loudly.

A little boy who wore the remains of an extraordinary black cap on his red hair and who carried the remains of a pair of spectacles at his waist, stepped forward, then changed his mind and stood still.

'We saw your smoke. And you don't know how many of you there are?'

'No, sir.'

'I should have thought,' said the officer as he visualised the search before him, 'I should have thought that a [6]pack of British boys – you're all British, aren't you? – would have been able to put up a better show than that – I mean –'

'It was like that at first,' said Ralph, 'before things –'

He stopped.

'We were together, then –'

The officer nodded helpfully.

---

a ⓘCircle the words or phrases which are closest in meaning to the underlined words in the text.

1 a (followed) b covered c hurt

2 a pair of scissors b small boat c sailor

3 a Smiling b Without speaking c Laughing

4 a smiled b shouted c waved

5 a for sure b as an officer c usually

6 a group b school c number

b Read the text again and answer the questions.

1 The officer takes his hand away from his revolver. Why do you think his hand was on the revolver?

2 When Ralph says 'Hullo', he answers an unspoken question. What do you think is the question?

3 The officer says 'Fun and games' and then he smiles. What does he think is happening?

4 Does the officer believe it when Ralph says two boys were killed? How do you know?

5 Ralph says 'before things –' but he doesn't finish the sentence. What do you think he was going to say?

Skills in mind

6 Write

Wanted – Samaritan of the Year

Do you have a colleague at work or school who is always ready to help out anyone in need? Is your next-door neighbour a tireless campaigner for charity? Do you know anyone who'd never say 'I'm sorry, I'm too busy'?

If your answer to any of these questions was 'yes', then you might just be the person to help us find our Samaritan of the Year.

Send us an email (no longer than 300 words), telling us who this person is and exactly why they deserve the title, and you could find yourself on the front page of our paper with your Samaritan.

And there's more. As well as instant fame, your Samaritan will win £1,000 to donate to a charity of his or her choice – so don't forget to tell us what this charity is and why your Samaritan has chosen it.

a What do you think a Samaritan is? Tick (✔) the best definition 1, 2 or 3. Read the advert to check.

1 someone who works for charity ☐

2 someone who helps other people ☐

3 a good friend ☐

b Read the advert again and <u>underline</u> four pieces of information that should be included in every competition entry.

c A student has written a reply to the competition advert. Read the email and answer the questions.

1 Who is Paul Scott?

2 Why is he being nominated?

3 What charity will the money go to and why?

This time last year I was sitting in my small London hotel room wondering if I would ever be able to adapt to my new home. I had come to the UK from Poland to start a new life. There was only one problem – I couldn't speak a word of English. Now, one year later, I have a great job, a new circle of friends and I couldn't be happier. All because one person took the time and care to help me learn my new language. Paul Scott is a professional English teacher. It is his job to help immigrants to the UK to learn English. But for Paul it is more than a job – it is a personal challenge to help each and every one of us. Besides the long hours he works in the classroom, Paul arranges extra lessons. Each student has his phone number and can call him whenever they have a problem. In the evenings and at the weekends, Paul arranges social activities for us. Paul is more than a teacher, he is a friend and he really cares. He knows how lonely life can be when you start living in a new country and he does all that he can to make the process easier. Paul is the friendly face of the UK, making all of us feel at home the moment we meet him, and for this reason I would like to nominate him for Samaritan of the Year.

If Paul wins, he will donate the money to New Home, a charity that works to help immigrants adapt to their new life, because it is a charity that has helped many people and Paul would like to give them something back.

d Write your entry for the competition.

WRITING TIP

Writing an entry for a competition

- As always, read through the instructions carefully and underline or highlight the key points. Make sure you answer all of these.

- It is good to use the key points to help you organise your writing. How and in what order are you going to answer them?

- Can you think of a way of making your entry stand out from the rest? Perhaps you could start with a funny story or a quotation. Or you could use anecdotes – little stories about your experiences. This will make your writing more personal and interesting to the reader.

Unit check

1 Fill in the spaces

Complete the text with the words in the box.

with	travelling	about	had	for
~~was~~	been	arrived	what	from

The very first Nobel Peace Prize ¹ _was_ awarded to Jean Henri Dunant, a Swiss businessman ² _____ Geneva. In 1859, Dunant's travels took him to the small town of Solferino, which today is in Italy. He had been ³ _____ all day when he ⁴ _____ and found that the town had ⁵ _____ the scene of a battle between Napoleon III's army and the Austrian army. More than 30,000 men ⁶ _____ been killed or seriously wounded. Dunant was shocked by ⁷ _____ he saw, and he decided to stay on to help ⁸ _____ the injured. He wrote ⁹ _____ his experiences in a book called *A Memory of Solferino*. This book became the inspiration ¹⁰ _____ the creation of the International Red Cross, whose mission is to protect human life and health.

9

2 Choose the correct answers

Circle the correct answer: a, b or c.

1 Do you know if Steve and Janice have made _____ yet or are they still not speaking?
   a to   b on   c (up)

2 All the seats had _____ taken so we had to stand.
   a be   b been   c being

3 Why do you always _____ his side in every argument?
   a go on   b make   c take

4 When we arrived we were exhausted because we _____ for nearly 15 hours.
   a had flown   b had flying   c had been flying

5 I've fallen _____ with my dad because he won't let me go to the party this weekend.
   a out   b on   c in

6 We were late and when we arrived at the party they _____ already _____ 'Happy Birthday'.
   a had sung   b have been singing   c had been singing

7 I'm a bit _____ with this problem and need some help.
   a caught   b stuck   c frozen

8 I think we need to _____ a few things out before we go any further.
   a sort   b decide   c mend

9 Their wedding cake _____ made by his mother. It was beautiful.
   a had   b has been   c had been

8

3 Vocabulary

Change the underlined words. Use the words in brackets.

1 I try not to <u>take sides</u> when mum and dad quarrel. **(neutral)**
   stay neutral

2 Bob and Amy <u>aren't speaking to each other</u>. **(fallen)** _____

3 It was a serious argument and they almost <u>started fighting</u>. **(blows)**
   _____

4 I think they're <u>friends again</u>. **(made)**
   _____

5 They've <u>found a solution which is OK for both of them</u>. **(compromise)**
   _____

6 The UN are doing all they can to find a way of <u>stopping the fighting</u>. **(resolve)** _____

7 My sisters <u>refuse to talk to each other</u>. **(terms)** _____

8 Tim always <u>looks for things to argue about</u>. **(pick)** _____

9 You and your dad need to <u>find a way of resolving</u> your problems. **(sort)** _____

8

How did you do?

Total: | 25 |

😊	Very good 20 – 25	😐	OK 14 – 19	😟	Review Unit 7 again 0 – 13

1 Grammar
✱ Dummy *it*

a Put the words in the correct order to make sentences.

1 to / it / lonely / feel / hurts
    It hurts to feel lonely.

2 wonderful / it's / kind / be / to
    ....

3 it / good / people / to / see / smile / feels
    ....

4 to / you're / it's / say / sorry / important
    ....

5 isn't / be / hard / it / nice / to / people / other / to
    ....

6 help / it / anything / cost / to / doesn't / people
    ....

7 stressed / not / unusual / to / who / are / see / people / it's
    ....

8 difficult / it's / don't / to / why / each / other / people / talk / to / understand
    ....
    ....

c Rewrite the sentences to start with *It*.

1 Cycling in the traffic? That's crazy!
    It's crazy to cycle in the traffic.

2 Having a good time in this town is hard.
    ....

3 Making new friends is fun.
    ....

4 Helping other people is nice.
    ....

5 Smiling doesn't hurt.
    ....

6 You forget people's names sometimes. That's normal.
    ....

7 Being kind to other people doesn't cost anything.
    ....

8 Seeing other people smile when you help them is wonderful.
    ....

b Match the sentences with the people in the pictures. Write 1–6 in the boxes.

1 It's difficult to see where we're going.
2 It's important to exchange our details.
3 It isn't easy to live in the city.
4 It's difficult to know which to get.
5 It's fun to try new things.
6 It's great to see you again!

2 Vocabulary

✱ Making an effort

a Complete the puzzle.

```
      8
 ¹ T  R  I  A  L
 ²
    ³
 ⁴
      ⁵
        ⁶
        ⁷
```

1 We were lost and we didn't have a map, but we found our way home by ___trial___ and error.

2 If I do a job, I always want to do it _____ .

3 My brother looked ashamed of himself, so I knew he'd done something _____ .

4 The instructions were really complicated and I _____ for hours to understand them.

5 I loved the drama classes and I think I got a lot _____ of doing them.

6 I wasn't really interested in the game, so I only played half-_____ .

7 I don't always find it _____ to solve problems.

8 My parents went to great _____ to pay for me to go to university.

b Complete the text with the expressions in the box. There is one expression you won't use.

> trial and error   ~~find it easy~~   got a lot out of it
> struggled   did the job properly   half-heartedly
> go to great lengths   done something wrong

Last week there was a problem with my computer. Now, I don't ¹ _find it easy_ to work with computers, but I will ² _____ not to spend money, so I decided to try to fix it myself. I ³ _____ to find out what the problem was, and finally I fixed it – not really with any knowledge, just by ⁴ _____ . But I must have ⁵ _____ because two days later, the problem was back – and worse! Although I knew I wouldn't be able to fix it, I tried ⁶ _____ for about an hour, but it was no good. So I called a computer technician, and he came round and ⁷ _____ .

c 【Vocabulary bank】 Complete the text with the correct form of the words in the box.

> sweat   bother   can
> ~~put~~   make   be

My husband ¹ _put_ everything into making our anniversary a day to remember. He spent hours ² _____ over the internet to find us somewhere special to eat. He ³ _____ a real attempt to dress up smartly, which is something I know he hates doing. He even ⁴ _____ to polish his shoes! And it ⁵ _____ really worth the effort because he looked great. Yes, my husband really tried his hardest to make things special. It's just a shame he ⁶ _____ be bothered to check the calendar and get the right day!

3 Pronunciation

✱ Connecting sounds (intrusive /w/ and /j/)

a Read the sentences aloud to yourself. Write *w* or *y*: *w* if the underlined sounds have a linking 'w' sound; *y* if they have a linking 'y' sound.

1 You and I have to talk about it.   _w_

2 Our uncle sent it for me and my sister.   _____

3 I think I'm too old to play those games.   _____

4 I wish he'd go away.   _____

5 It's the easiest thing to do.   _____

6 She used to study more.   _____

b ▶ CD4 T15 Listen and check. Then listen again and repeat.

4 Grammar

✳ Modals review

a Match the sentences 1–8 with the explanations a–h.

1 We couldn't leave school before we were 16.
2 I think it'll rain tomorrow.
3 I must remember to phone her today.
4 You could try being nice to people.
5 May I borrow your newspaper?
6 It must have been difficult to live in the 19th century.
7 I've invited him, but he might not come.
8 I could already play the violin when I was eight.

a making a prediction
b asking for permission
c talking about a possible future event
d expressing a past prohibition
e talking about ability in the past
f expressing an obligation
g making a deduction about the past
h making a suggestion

b Underline the correct words.

1 I'm not sure yet, but I *will / might* go to Spain for my birthday.
2 Let's give him a book – he*'ll / can* like that.
3 If we don't go to her party, she*'ll / 'd* feel awful.
4 She's a terrible dancer – you *shouldn't / won't* dance with her.
5 I forgot her birthday last year, so I *must / can't* forget it again this year.
6 I'm sorry I forgot, but I promise I*'ll / should* get you a present tomorrow.
7 Thank you for the present – *can / will* I open it now?
8 Well, we haven't been invited to the party, so I think we *couldn't / shouldn't* go.

c Underline the correct verb to complete each dialogue.

1 'What am I going to get my dad for his birthday?'
   'Well, he likes music, so I think you *may / should* get him a CD.'
2 'Jill's going to be 19 next week.'
   'That *can't / shouldn't* be right – she's still at school!'
3 'Did you like the book I gave you? I haven't read it myself yet.'
   'Yes, it's wonderful – you really *can / must* read it.'
4 'I'm going to the shop to get stuff for the party.'
   'OK – *can / would* I come with you?'
5 'I wonder how old our teacher is.'
   'Well, you *won't / mustn't* ask her, she might not like it.'
6 'My grandfather's 75 next week, and he's throwing a party.'
   'Great. If I were 75, I *won't / wouldn't* have the energy for a party!'

d Complete what each person is saying with an appropriate modal verb. There is sometimes more than one possible answer.

1 I ＿＿＿＿＿＿ find that ring!
2 Excuse me. ＿＿＿＿ I use your phone?
3 No, that ＿＿＿＿＿ be the right way to do it!
4 I'm not sure, but I think they ＿＿＿＿＿ be tourists!
5 I ＿＿＿＿＿ do that if you paid me – I'm much too scared!
6 You ＿＿＿＿＿ have eaten too much at the restaurant.

5 Read

a Read the text about Annie Lennox. Some lines have an extra word which should not be there. If the line is correct, put a tick (✓). If a word should not be there, cross it out and write the word at the end of the line.

Annie Lennox began her recording career as the lead singer of the British	1	✓
pop band The Tourists but after three years and only moderate success	2	*has*
she has left with band mate Dave Stewart to form the duo Eurythmics. It was	3	
with Eurythmics that Annie who began to enjoy a considerable amount of	4	
recognition not only in the UK but also in many countries around of the world.	5	
In the 1990s Annie embarked on a solo career and continued where	6	
Eurythmics left off with several bestselling albums. In 2010 she released her	7	
fifth solo album. She has won a number of music awards which including eight	8	
BRIT awards, a Golden Globe and an Oscar for 'Into the West' which she	9	
wrote for the soundtrack to *The Lord of the Rings*.	10	
As well as having been a hugely successful career as a musician, Annie is	11	
also a political and social activist, working tirelessly for more better health	12	
awareness in Africa, and campaigning for the peace in the Middle East.	13	

b Read the text again. Mark the statements *T* (true) or *F* (false). Correct the false statements.

1 Annie Lennox has been in three bands.
2 The Tourists were a very popular band.
3 Eurythmics were not only popular in the UK.
4 Annie won an Oscar for her role in *The Lord of the Rings*.
5 Annie is involved in issues outside of pop music.

c ▶ **CD4 T16** Listen to the biography of Al Green and answer the questions.

1 What success did Al Green have as a child?

2 What success did Al Green have in the early 1970s?

3 What two incidents had a major effect on Al Green's life?

4 How did they change his life?

5 When did he return to recording popular music?

6 What kind of records does he make these days?

6 Listen

a ▶ **CD4 T17** Listen to the story and put the pictures in the correct order.

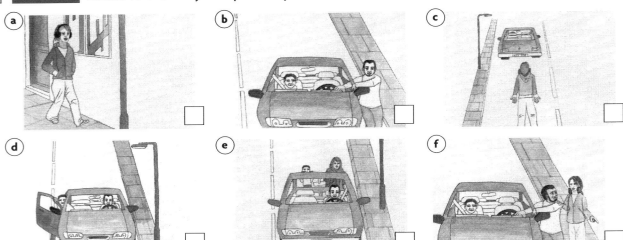

b ▶ **CD4 T17** Listen again and answer the questions.

1 Where was the speaker going, and what was he going to do?

....

2 What was the title of the song he was listening to?

....

3 Why was the man pushing his car?

....

4 How old was the small boy?

....

5 How far did they push the car?

....

6 Why was the speaker so surprised at the end?

....

LISTENING TIP

Listening to stories

When you listen to someone telling a story or an anecdote in a casual conversation, you'll notice many important things that can help you understand better.

- The verb tense that the person uses might be past, or it might be present, or it might be a mixture of both. Which is it in this story?

- The person telling the story hasn't usually planned what to say, so sometimes he or she will start to say something, then start again in a different way. Can you hear examples of this in the story?

- If it's a casual conversation, you'll often hear people use 'fillers' – sounds or words which give them a little time to think. In English, these are things like *erm, you know* or *kind of.* Listen to the story and notice when this happens.

- The person telling the story will sometimes mention things which are not very important, before going back to the main points of the story. The word *anyway* is often used to show that the story is going back to what's important. Listen to the story again and see how the speaker does this here.

Unit check

1 Fill in the spaces

Complete the text with the words in the box.

| arguments | wrong | struggled | half-heartedly | ~~important~~ | lengths | properly | must | find | couldn't |

I know that it's [1] _important_ to have friends and be nice to them, but I don't always [2] _____ it easy. A few weeks ago, for example, I was really angry with a friend of mine and shouted at her. Normally I hate [3] _____ and I go to great [4] _____ not to argue, but this time I just [5] _____ avoid it, especially because I felt that I hadn't done anything [6] _____. I'd borrowed a DVD from this friend and after I'd given it back she said that I hadn't looked after it [7] _____ because it was scratched. She said I [8] _____ have left it lying around, which of course wasn't true at all. I [9] _____ to keep my temper, but I didn't succeed and in the end we just shouted at each other. The next day she apologised, but very [10] _____, so I didn't really believe her. I guess I need to learn how to deal with people better!

[9]

2 Choose the correct answers

Circle the correct answer: a, b or c.

1 I don't find _____ easy to meet new people.
   a the   b (it)   c them

2 They went to _____ lengths to help me.
   a great   b big   c long

3 Sometimes the best way to find the answer is through trial and _____.
   a mistake   b result   c error

4 I don't really like dancing, so if I dance at all, I dance _____-heartedly.
   a semi   b part   c half

5 You paid £25.00 for this CD? You _____ be crazy!
   a must   b can't   c can

6 _____ I borrow your pen, please?
   a May   b Will   c Should

7 The sky's very dark – I think it _____ rain later this afternoon.
   a would   b must   c will

8 I know it's bad news, but I think we _____ tell him anyway.
   a should   b would   c can't

9 If you come to Britain, you _____ come and visit us. We'd love to see you!
   a will   b must   c may

[8]

3 Vocabulary

Underline the correct words.

1 They made the discovery by trial and mistake / _error_ / fault.

2 I loved maths at school. Probably because I made / did / found it really easy.

3 Did you say 'thank you'? He went to great / long / problems / lengths to get that present for you.

4 Being a nurse doesn't pay a lot but I get a lot out from / of / by helping people.

5 I passed the exam no sweat / tears / difficult. It was really easy.

6 Thank you for your application. We will be / succeed / endeavour to contact you by the end of the week.

7 You've been sweating on / with / over that homework for hours. Take a break.

8 He put everything on / into / over making her a birthday card and she didn't even read it.

9 I can't be worried / bothered / troubled to go out tonight. I'm too tired.

[8]

How did you do?

Total: [25]

| 😊 | Very good 20 – 25 | 😐 | OK 14 – 19 | 😞 | Review Unit 8 again 0 – 13 |

1 Grammar

❋ Phrasal verbs

a Match the sentences with the pictures.

1 He's always taking off his father.

2 You won't get away with this!

3 Hmm. I'm not sure which one to go for.

4 I wonder what Jenkins has come up with this time.

5 It's awful when they take off.

6 I'm not sure what it is. Why don't you look it up in that book?

b Circle the correct phrasal verb in brackets. Then complete the sentence with the correct form of the verb.

1 I don't know who did this, but I'm going to __find out__ ! ((find out) / come across)

2 The good weather has _____ an increase in bumble bees this summer. (*bring about / take off*)

3 How can I _____ it _____ in a dictionary if I don't know how to spell it? (*come across / look up*)

4 If I were you I would _____ the most expensive one. (*come up with / go for*)

5 I _____ some old letters from my gran while I was tidying up the attic. (*come across / find out*)

6 The plane _____ at 4 o'clock so we have to leave by ten. (*take off / go for*)

7 She's always late for school but the teachers never say anything – I don't know how she _____ it! (*come up with / get away with*)

8 He's _____ a great new idea for tidying his bedroom quickly – hide it all under the bed! (*come up with / get away with*)

c Put the words in order to make sentences or questions.

1 late / plane / the / hours / off / took / two
   The plane took off two hours late.

2 out / I'm / trying / find / to
   _____

3 rude / being / with / away / they / got
   _____

4 should / dress / which / for / do / think / you / I / go
   _____ ?

5 would / £1,000 / about / problems / an / bring / end / my / to / all
   _____

6 bit / across / comes / as / a / being / superficial / she
   _____

7 means / I / it / know / but / I / what / up / still / don't / looked / it
   _____

8 that / came / idea / who / with / up / great
   _____ ?

d Rewrite the sentences using *it* or *them* instead of the underlined noun. Change the word order if necessary.

1 She went for the salmon.

   She went for it.

2 I never found out the answers to my problems.

   ----

3 I came across the coins in my garden.

   ----

4 I got away with not doing my homework.

   ----

5 I looked up the word in my dictionary.

   ----

6 He came up with the idea in the bath.

   ----

2 Vocabulary

a Complete the sentences with a phrasal verb from the box. Use the correct form of the verb. You may use some of the verbs more than once.

> go for   look up   work out
> come across   take off

1 His plane ___took off___ at eleven last night.

2 They were having some problems but things are starting to _____ for them.

3 If we're eating out I'll always _____ Indian food.

4 It was a great idea and it _____ immediately.

5 What a lovely bird. Let's _____ it _____ in the guide.

6 I _____ an old book of yours while I was sorting out my bookcase.

7 They _____ as being really unfriendly but they're just a bit shy.

8 He's great at _____ all the teachers at our school. It's really funny.

9 I just wanted to stroke the dog but it really _____ me.

b Vocabulary bank Complete the crossword.

Across

1 The language used by deaf people.

3 Very informal language.

4 This language is rude and offensive.

6 Words and phrases used by groups of people (scientists, etc.), especially in the workplace.

Down

1 A phrase that is easy to remember, often used in advertising.

2 Terminology that is annoying.

3 To use bad language.

5 An expression that is very often used, so it's not original or interesting.

7 A group of words that has a specific meaning.

3 Pronunciation

-ough /uː/, /ʌ/, /ɒ/ or /əʊ/

a Draw lines between the words ending in *-ough* and the words they sound like.

-ough sounds	sounds like…
enough	blue /uː/
through	stu**ff** /ʌ/
tough	kn**ow** /əʊ/
cough	**o**ff /ɒ/
though	
rough	

b ▶ CD4 T18 Listen and check.

c ▶ CD4 T19 Listen and repeat.

1 I didn't have enough money though.

2 That's a nasty cough you've got.

3 This steak is tough right through.

4 The sea's not rough enough for surfing.

4 Vocabulary

✳ Understanding language

a Complete the sentences with the words in the box.

get   out   ~~make~~   lost   gist   totally

1 I can't _make_ out a
   word of it.

2 Well, I didn't get all
   of it but I think I got
   the _____ .

3 I'm sorry, you _____
   me completely at the
   second 'click'.

4 Is it just me or is
   my dad _____
   incomprehensible?

5 I can pick _____ a
   couple of words. This
   might be 'crocodile' but
   I'm not 100% sure.

6 I don't really _____
   it.

b Put the words in order to make
   sentences.

1 lost / completely / me / he's
   He's completely lost me.

2 understand / to / managing / it /
   most / I'm / of
   _____

3 I / the / gist / about / just / can /
   catch
   _____
   _____

4 saying / I / lot / understand / a /
   of / what / he's
   _____
   _____

5 can't / I / make / much / very / out
   _____
   _____

6 incomprehensible / totally / the /
   he / gives / are / talks
   _____
   _____

c Match two of the sentences in
   Exercise 4b with each of the people
   in the picture.

1 A might say sentences ____ and ____ .

2 B might say sentences _2_ and ____ .

3 C might say sentences ____ and ____ .

5 Culture in mind

a Rupert A. H. Barnes has invented his own language.
Read his introduction to it and find out what it's called.

When a student gets frustrated with the oddities and illogicalities of French and German he or she might give up. Alternatively he or she might become interested in linguistics. I became interested in linguistics. It has been many years since my schooldays but I have stayed interested.

Artificial languages are a minor area of linguistics. There are, however, a phenomenal number of artificial languages around. Indeed, while natural languages are shrinking in number, man-made ones are increasing. Of course, there might be just one speaker, or none, of any given man-made tongue.

There are many reasons for someone to want to devise an artificial language, and many people have done so. I have written one myself. I've called it Bannzish. One man might want to find a way for all the peoples of the world to talk together in peace in a common language. For another it is an intellectual exercise to keep the brain exercising. Another treats it as an amusement, to fill the time. Yet another has it as a way to take his frustrations out on his very words, trying to force an order on them and enjoying some kind of power over them.

My reasons are all of those except the first. The whole idea is ridiculous. Who could think the French would want to abandon the language of Voltaire or the Germans the speech of Goethe? I would certainly not give up the tongue of Shakespeare and Dickens. I have none of those silly delusions which support, for example, Esperanto. Instead I enjoy being pleased with myself for being bright enough to have a good go at the man-made language game. The doing of it has also taught me a lot more of depth about the several languages I already knew and brought a new appreciation for English itself.

No exercise like this is ever finished. The English language is still unfinished after 1,500 years of use. I found, as will you if you do the same, that I was always coming up with new logical problems and having to think of new subtleties. I am a determined sort, and once I started my little intellectual exercise I could not stop until the end, which never came. Language is not a simple matter. Perhaps the old, illogical, irregular but real languages are better after all. Do not let that stop you from trying the same, though, if you are thinking about it.

b Read the text again and (circle) the correct answer: a, b, c or d.

1 What experience of learning language did the author have at school?

  a He found it boring.

  b He developed a great interest in language which has lasted all his life.

  c He became fluent in both French and German.

  d He only realised how interesting languages were later on in his life.

2 Which of these differences between artificial and natural language does the writer <u>not</u> make?

  a Natural languages are more important.

  b Natural languages are spoken by many more people.

  c The number of natural languages in the world is falling.

  d Natural languages are much older than artificial ones.

3 Which of these was not a reason for the author to invent his own language?

  a To try and create a language to bring people together.

  b As an intellectual exercise.

  c For fun.

  d As a way of trying to control language.

4 What is his main criticism of Esperanto?

  a It is designed only for speakers of French and German.

  b It is far too complicated.

  c It is unrealistic and self-important.

  d It is badly thought out.

5 What has the writer's experience taught him?

  a It takes a long time to finish a language.

  b No language is perfect.

  c Natural languages are better.

  d Don't waste your time writing an artificial language.

6 Read

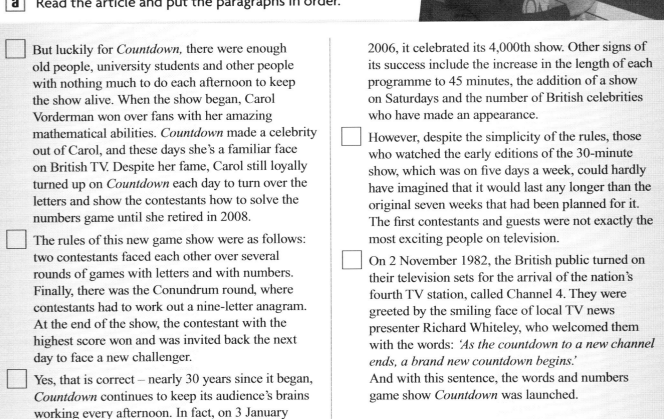

a Read the article and put the paragraphs in order.

☐ But luckily for *Countdown,* there were enough old people, university students and other people with nothing much to do each afternoon to keep the show alive. When the show began, Carol Vorderman won over fans with her amazing mathematical abilities. *Countdown* made a celebrity out of Carol, and these days she's a familiar face on British TV. Despite her fame, Carol still loyally turned up on *Countdown* each day to turn over the letters and show the contestants how to solve the numbers game until she retired in 2008.

☐ The rules of this new game show were as follows: two contestants faced each other over several rounds of games with letters and with numbers. Finally, there was the Conundrum round, where contestants had to work out a nine-letter anagram. At the end of the show, the contestant with the highest score won and was invited back the next day to face a new challenger.

☐ Yes, that is correct – nearly 30 years since it began, *Countdown* continues to keep its audience's brains working every afternoon. In fact, on 3 January

2006, it celebrated its 4,000th show. Other signs of its success include the increase in the length of each programme to 45 minutes, the addition of a show on Saturdays and the number of British celebrities who have made an appearance.

☐ However, despite the simplicity of the rules, those who watched the early editions of the 30-minute show, which was on five days a week, could hardly have imagined that it would last any longer than the original seven weeks that had been planned for it. The first contestants and guests were not exactly the most exciting people on television.

☐ On 2 November 1982, the British public turned on their television sets for the arrival of the nation's fourth TV station, called Channel 4. They were greeted by the smiling face of local TV news presenter Richard Whiteley, who welcomed them with the words: *'As the countdown to a new channel ends, a brand new countdown begins.'*
And with this sentence, the words and numbers game show *Countdown* was launched.

b Read the text again. Mark the statements *T* (true) or *F* (false). Correct the false statements.

1 *Countdown* was the first programme ever shown on Channel 4. ☐

2 Originally only 35 programmes of *Countdown* were planned. ☐

3 The early shows were popular with working people. ☐

4 Carol Vorderman is no longer involved with the show. ☐

5 These days *Countdown* is on for four and a half hours every week. ☐

6 Every day two new contestants compete to become *Countdown* champion. ☐

READING TIP

Putting paragraphs in order

- First read through all the text quickly.
- Next highlight the first line of each paragraph, which provides a link back to the previous paragraph.
- From your highlighted sentences, find the one which is the beginning of the text as a whole.
- Read carefully through your first paragraph and make sure you understand what it is talking about. Then look at your other first lines. Which one refers back to the topics mentioned in the opening paragraph?
- Repeat this process until you have all the paragraphs in order.
- Finally, read carefully through the text using the paragraph order you have chosen. This is your final check to see if it really makes sense.

Unit check

1 Fill in the spaces

Complete the text with the words in the box.

speaks paid to speak get which
to speaking make ~~worst~~ would trying

The English are often said to be the ^{1} _worst_ language learners in the world. They think that because everyone else ^{2} _____ English, they don't need to learn any other languages. When it comes ^{3} _____ languages – I'm terrible. In my German lessons at school I ^{4} _____ spend most of the time ^{5} _____ not to fall asleep. Now I live in Germany I wish I had ^{6} _____ more attention. When I try ^{7} _____ German I don't think people can ^{8} _____ out much of what I say. And when people speak to me, I'm lucky if I can just ^{9} _____ the gist. Of course, because most Germans speak English well, they soon start speaking it, ^{10} _____ means I never practise speaking German! [9]

2 Choose the correct answers

(Circle) the correct answer: a, b or c.

1 She talks so fast that I can't even _____ the gist.
   a (get) b find c see

2 I would _____ for a notebook. They're much easier to carry around with you..
   a select b choose c go

3 Many idioms are _____ incomprehensible until you learn what they mean.
   a very b totally c so

4 I _____ to pick out a few words.
   a managed b could c able

5 He got into trouble for taking _____ his headmaster in the lesson.
   a in b up c off

6 My younger brother gets _____ with everything. It's not fair.
   a away b off c about

7 You've _____ me completely. What exactly are we talking about?
   a caught b missed c lost

8 My dad found _____ that I went to the party. He was furious.
   a on b out c away

9 I _____ most of what she said but not everything.
   a picked b got c listened [8]

3 Vocabulary

Complete the sentences with the missing words. The first letter has been given.

1 My doctor uses so much medical
   j a r g o n , it's difficult to
   understand him sometimes.

2 Don't talk with food in your mouth.
   I didn't understand a w _ _ _ _ of what you just said.

3 I _ _ _ _ _ _ are the hardest things to understand. Their meanings are often so different to the words in them.

4 I got the g _ _ _ of what he said but I didn't understand everything.

5 My dad s _ _ _ _ _ _ a lot when he watches football. He uses such bad language.

6 The teenagers I met in the UK spoke so much s _ _ _ _ that I couldn't understand them.

7 When we were in Peru I managed to m _ _ _ out a few words of Spanish.

8 She's deaf so she uses s _ _ _ _ language to communicate.

9 I got a letter from my lawyer. I don't understand a word of it. It's
   i _ _ _ _ _ _ _ _ _ _ _ _ _ _ _ _ _ .

[8]

How did you do?

Total: [25]

| :) Very good 20 – 25 | :| OK 14 – 19 | :(Review Unit 9 again 0 – 13 |

1 Grammar

✳ Reduced relative clauses

a Read the text. At the end of each line, put a tick (✔) if the underlined words are needed or a cross (✘) if the underlined words are not needed.

Roger Federer, [1] who is a top *ATP player and a strong supporter of children's charities, became a UNICEF Goodwill Ambassador in April 2006. Like other Goodwill Ambassadors such as David Beckham and Youssou N'dour, Federer will work to support UNICEF in its efforts to bring attention and resources to children around the world [2] who need help.

1 ✘

2 _____

'I am happy to become one of UNICEF's Goodwill Ambassadors,' Federer said. 'I've been lucky in life, and able to play tennis seriously since I was six years old. It's important to me to help the many children throughout the world [3] who do not have the everyday things they need.'

3 _____

Federer has used his success in tennis to remind the world that children are important. In 2003, he started the Roger Federer Foundation, [4] which raises money for disadvantaged children, mainly in South Africa (where his mother was brought up), and to promote sports for young people.

4 _____

After the terrible tsunami of 2004, Federer started several fund-raising campaigns, including the ATP 'All-Star Rally for Relief', a tennis event [5] which was supported by many of the top men and women players. All the money [6] that was raised went to UNICEF.

5 _____

6 _____

That event started a worldwide partnership between the ATP and UNICEF called ACE ('Assisting Children Everywhere'), [7] which aims to use the power of tennis to help provide health, education and protection to the poor children of the world.

7 _____

*ATP = Association of Tennis Professionals

---

b In each sentence, write ↑ in the place where the relative pronoun and the verb are missing. Then write the missing words at the end of the sentence.

1 Coldplay performed a song ↑ called *Christmas Lights* ____which was____

2 Here is an extract taken from the first chapter of the book. _____

3 The Great Sphinx is a famous statue, half-human, half-lion, built by the Egyptians. _____

4 Harry Potter is a fictional character created by J. K. Rowling. _____

5 The A380 plane, built by Airbus Industries, can seat over 550 passengers. _____

6 The Live 8 concert attended by 15,000 people was a success. _____

2 Vocabulary

✳ Fame

a Circle the correct word: a, b or c.

1 He's famous _____ making fun of politicians.
   a from   b (for)   c by

2 Some people _____ a name for themselves by doing crazy things.
   a have   b do   c make

3 Her career started slowly, but then she really _____ it big in 2004.
   a made   b did   c hit

4 Roger Federer is such a successful tennis player that now he's a _____ name.
   a house   b home   c household

5 Not many people know her now, but she _____ a lot of success back in the 1990s.
   a made   b enjoyed   c liked

6 Kylie Minogue became a singing _____ a few years ago.
   a sensation   b sense   c excitement

b Complete the text with words from Exercise 2a.

John McEnroe was an American tennis player in the 1980s and 1990s who became famous ¹ _for_ shouting at umpires and throwing his racket around. Born in 1959, he was a teenage tennis ² _____

who won the French junior championship at the age of only 18. Later in 1977, he reached the semi-finals at Wimbledon and became a ³ _____ name all over the world. He really ⁴ _____ it big in 1979 when he won the US Open title in front of his home crowd. By that time, he had also ⁵ _____ a name for himself as a player who regularly lost his temper and shouted at opponents and officials. His most famous phrase was 'You cannot be serious!'

After he retired from playing tennis in 1992, McEnroe ⁶ _____ a lot of success as a TV tennis commentator.

3 Vocabulary

✻ Expressing your opinion

a Complete the sentences with the words in the box.

> ask   mind   concerned
> thought   way   ~~opinion~~

1 In my _opinion_ , celebrities should keep out of politics.

2 I'd have _____ that film stars could help quite a lot with world problems.

3 The _____ I see it, poor people need help from anywhere in the world.

4 As far as I'm _____ , the celebrities just want publicity for themselves.

5 To my _____ , celebrities should do as much as they can to help charities.

6 If you _____ me, footballers are the best people to be Goodwill Ambassadors.

b Put the words in the correct order to make expressions that give opinions.

1 for / I'm / all / it   ☐
  I'm all for it.

2 less / care / couldn't / I   ☐
  _____

3 matter / it / really / doesn't   ☐
  _____

4 not / it's / a / idea / good   ☐
  _____

5 against / completely / I'm / it   ☐
  _____

6 thing / it / be / can't / a / bad   ☐
  _____

c Next to each expression in Exercise 3b, write a tick (✔) if it gives a positive opinion, a cross (✘) if it gives a negative opinion, or ∅ if it gives a neutral opinion.

d **Vocabulary bank** Complete the sentences with the words in the box.

> express   high   difference   public
> ~~matter~~   poll   considered   second

1 It depends who you talk to – it's a _matter_ of opinion, really.

2 It's unusual for Jack not to say anything. He usually loves to _____ his opinion.

3 I've thought long and hard about your proposal and it's my _____ opinion that we should do it.

4 Let's not argue. Let's agree that we have a _____ of opinion.

5 If you're not happy with what the doctor said, you should definitely get a _____ opinion.

6 Lucy thinks she's so great. She's got such a _____ opinion of herself.

7 The government hasn't got a chance in the elections if you believe the latest opinion _____ .

8 The government wants to take us to war even though _____ opinion is against it.

4 Grammar

✱ Question tags review

a Some of these question tags are incorrect. If
the question tag is correct, write a tick (✔).
If the question tag is incorrect, write a cross (✘)
and the correct tag.

1 It's an important issue, isn't it? ✔

2 Harry Potter's known all over the world, isn't it?
✘   *isn't he?*

3 You aren't sure what to do, do you? ☐
----

4 Angelina Jolie works for UNICEF, don't she?
☐ --------------------------------

5 He went to Africa to see the problem, hasn't he?
☐ --------------------------------

6 She must have made a lot of money, mustn't
she? ☐ --------------------------------

7 The film didn't do very well, didn't it? ☐
----

8 They enjoyed a lot of success in the 1990s,
weren't they? ☐ --------------------------------

9 He's really made a name for himself, hasn't he?
☐ --------------------------------

10 They couldn't raise enough money, could they?
☐ --------------------------------

b Complete the sentences with the correct
question tags.

1 They don't help out very much, *do they?*

2 It's boring to read about all these film stars,
-------------------- ?

3 They haven't enjoyed much success,
-------------------- ?

4 She doesn't mind being famous,
-------------------- ?

5 She'll do anything to get more publicity,
-------------------- ?

6 They tried everything they could to help,
-------------------- ?

7 We should try to raise money for them,
-------------------- ?

8 They couldn't get help to all the starving people,
-------------------- ?

c Complete the dialogue with the
correct question tags.

Harry: Did you see the programme about
celebrity charity work last night?

Carol: Yes, it was interesting,
[1] *wasn't it?*

Harry: Not really. It didn't tell you much
you didn't already know,
[2] -------------------- ?

Carol: What do you mean?

Harry: I mean, we know everything there
is to know about Brad Pitt,
[3] -------------------- ? People don't want
to see his face on TV again,
[4] -------------------- ?

Carol: Oh, Harry – you can be really
boring sometimes.

Harry: Sorry, but you asked me what I
thought.

Carol: Well, yes – but if you always talk
like that, people won't ask you for your
opinion very often, [5] -------------------- ?

Harry: OK, I'm sorry. Let's talk about
something else. I mean we shouldn't
fall out over something as silly as this.

Carol: But Harry, you don't really think
charity work's silly, [6] -------------------- ?

d ▶ CD4 T20 Listen and check.

5 Pronunciation

✳ Intonation in question tags

a ▶ **CD4 T21** Listen to the sentences. For each one, write A if the person is asking a real question to check information (the voice goes up at the end), or B if the person is just trying to start a conversation (the voice goes down at the end).

1 You're new here, aren't you? _B_

2 You speak French, don't you? _A_

3 I'm being boring, aren't I? _____

4 It was an interesting programme, wasn't it? _____

5 You didn't enjoy it very much, did you? _____

6 This is a great party, isn't it? _____

7 They won't be late, will they? _____

8 You don't like this kind of music, do you? _____

b ▶ **CD4 T21** Listen again and repeat.

6 Everyday English

a Put the words in order to make phrases.

1 bet / I _____ _I bet_ _____

2 well / as / might / we

_____

3 reckon / you / do / what ?

_____

4 out / it / leave _____

5 less / I / care / couldn't

_____

6 much / I / as / thought

_____

b Which of the expressions in Exercise 6a means ...

a What's your opinion? _3_

b Can you stop doing (or saying) that? _____

c I can't see any reason why we shouldn't. _____

d I'm certain. _____

e I really don't have an opinion about that. _____

f That doesn't surprise me. _____

c Complete the dialogue with the expressions in Exercise 6a.

Lucy: Have you heard that Tim Bowen is going to release a book about his life in politics?

Oliver: [1] _____ . I mean I can't think of anything less interesting.

Lucy: Don't be so rude. I think it's quite exciting. He promises that he's going to paint a picture of what life is really like when you're prime minister.

Oliver: [2] _____ he doesn't say anything that we don't already know.

Lucy: Well, perhaps you should read a copy before you express your opinion about it. [3] _____ ?

Oliver: I don't need to. These politicians are all the same. They're only interested in talking about themselves. They don't really care about us.

Lucy: [4] _____ , Oliver. He wasn't a bad prime minister and he has done a lot of good around the world since he retired. In fact he's giving all the money he makes from the book to help education in Africa.

Oliver: Well, he doesn't need it. I mean he's not exactly short of money. If he sold some of the houses he owns or gave half his salary to charity, I might be impressed. He's just using his charity work to keep himself in the public eye. In case we forget about him.

Lucy: Wow, you're really not a fan of his, are you?

Oliver: No, not really.

Lucy: [5] _____ .

Oliver: Well, when you've read the book, maybe you can persuade me otherwise.

Lucy: I don't think I can be bothered.

Oliver: You're right. We always disagree, so [6] _____ not talk about politics any more.

Lucy: Good idea.

7 Listen

a ▶ **CD4 T22** Listen to an interview with an expert about UNICEF. Mark the statements *T* (true) or *F* (false).

1 UNICEF's ambassadors include photographers.   `T`

2 A Goodwill Ambassador's commitment begins when s/he starts working for UNICEF.   ☐

3 Youssou N'Dour became an ambassador in 1987.   ☐

4 Shakira had already worked in the area of children's education.   ☐

5 The two important things about ambassadors are: they get attention and they make decisions.   ☐

6 UNICEF wants children to have health, education, equality and protection.   ☐

7 Danny Kaye became Ambassador at Large in 1954.   ☐

8 Audrey Hepburn was also Ambassador at Large.   ☐

b ▶ **CD4 T22** Listen again and answer the questions.

1 What do all UNICEF's celebrities share?

----

2 Before he became a UNICEF ambassador, Youssou N'Dour took part in an immunisation programme. What else did he do?

----

3 Why is it important that UNICEF's ambassadors have access to politicians?

----

4 Why do politicians sometimes not pay much attention to children?

EXAM TIP

Before you listen and do a task

- Good preparation is very important, especially for a listening task. You might not have time to read through all the questions before you listen. But try to read and really think about as many of the questions as possible.

- With true / false tasks, like in Exercise 6a, read each sentence and consider what could be true or false about it. Key words will help you again.

- With open-ended questions, like in Exercise 6b, read and again decide what the key words are. For example, in the first sentence, the key words are *celebrities* and *share*. You might not hear these exact words when you listen: what other words might you hear?

Unit check

1 Fill in the spaces

Complete the text with the words in the box.

enjoying	won't	~~myself~~	see	concerned
will	bad	make	borrowed	household

I've always dreamed of making a real name for ¹ _myself_ in the music industry. I decided to get started with a guitar ² _____ from a friend, who said: 'I really love that guitar, so you'll give it back to me, ³ _____ you?' 'Sure,' I said. 'When I ⁴ _____ it big, I'll give it back to you!' He looked a bit worried. 'Look,' I said, 'the way I ⁵ _____ it, in a year or two I'm going to be a ⁶ _____ name! I'm going to be rich! Then I'll buy you all the guitars you want.'

'Well,' he said, 'I guess that can't be a ⁷ _____ thing. But listen – when you're ⁸ _____ all that success, you won't forget that I helped you, ⁹ _____ you?'

'It's OK, Jack,' I replied. 'As far as I'm ¹⁰ _____ , you're the best friend I've ever had, and of course I won't forget you.' He looked me in the eye. 'My name isn't Jack – it's Joe!' He took the guitar back, and that was the end of my musical career.

	9

2 Choose the correct answers

Ⓒircle the correct answer: a, b or c.

1 They really _____ in 2003 with their first CD.
   a made it large   b ⓑmade it big   c did it big

2 You won't tell anyone, _____ you?
   a will   b won't   c shall

3 Their last record didn't _____ a lot of success.
   a make   b win   c enjoy

4 A holiday in Spain? I'm all _____ it!
   a with   b on   c for

5 He hasn't phoned you, _____ he?
   a had   b hasn't   c has

6 To my _____ , UNICEF does great work all over the world.
   a mind   b view   c thought

7 The weren't very famous, _____ they?
   a are   b were   c weren't

8 I'd have _____ that the money could be spent in better ways.
   a concerned   b asked   c thought

9 They didn't pay you, _____ they?
   a do   b did   c didn't

	8

3 Vocabulary

Change the underlined words. Use the words in brackets.

1 To my mind they got what they deserved. (concerned)
   As far as I'm concerned

2 He became famous by winning a reality TV show. (name)
   _____

3 They didn't agree. (difference)
   _____

4 Why don't you ask another doctor what he thinks? (second)
   _____

5 If you ask me, they were both wrong. (way) _____

6 He really does think he's great. (high)
   _____

7 Everyone knows him. (household)
   _____

8 He had a lot of success in Japan. (big)
   _____

9 He was very successful for a few years. (enjoyed) _____

	8

How did you do?

Total: | 25 |

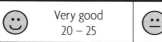 Very good
20 – 25

 OK
14 – 19

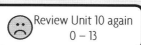 Review Unit 10 again
0 – 13

11 Music is everywhere

1 Grammar
✳ Indirect questions

a Put the words in the correct order to make indirect questions.

1 you / can / where / tell / post office / me / is / the

   Can you tell me where the post office is?

2 you / much / costs / do / how / this / know

   ----

3 tell / us / starts / you / what / film / can / the / time

   ----

4 you / can / him / test / he / what / mark / got / ask / in / the

   ----

5 arrived / you / when / know / do / they

   ----

6 speak / know / can / you / who / I / to / do

   ----

7 you / them / teacher / will / be / tell / who / the / can

   ----

8 is / you / name / what / know / do / his

   ----

b Write the indirect questions in Exercise 1a as direct questions.

1 *Where is the post office?*

2 --

3 --

4 --

5 --

6 --

7 --

8 --

c Anne Jacobs has an unusual job. She is responsible for choosing the music to play at Globo Gym in London. Read the interview with her and match the questions with the replies.

1 What kind of music do you play at the gym? | f |

2 What type of music is popular in the early mornings, for example? | |

3 What did you play this morning when you opened the gym? | |

4 What do people like to listen to while they exercise in the afternoons? | |

5 What time does it start getting busy again? | |

6 And what kind of music can we hear then? | |

7 How many clients has the gym got at the moment? | |

8 And how many complaints have you had about the music you play? | |

a None, incredibly. I guess I must be doing something right.

b Well, that's usually our busiest time, so something upbeat is good to get our clients moving and ready for the working day.

c Let me see. Yes, I remember. It was a collection of remixed songs by Madonna, Girls Aloud and people like that.

d The gym starts filling up around 6 pm with people dropping in on their way home from work.

e Over 500, I think.

f All types. It depends on the time of the day.

g After lunch is our quietest time of the day so we usually play slower, more relaxing music. Chill-out music, for example.

h Rock's pretty popular in the early evening. It helps people get in the mood for a night out.

d Make the questions in Exercise 1c indirect questions.

1 Can you tell us *what kind of music you play at the gym?*

2 Can you tell us _____ ?

3 Do you remember _____ ?

4 Can you tell us _____ ?

5 Do you know _____ ?

6 Can you tell us _____ ?

7 Do you know _____ ?

8 Can you tell us _____ ?

2 Vocabulary

✱ Making comparisons stronger

a At the Glastonbury music festival, Jenny saw several bands. Put the bands she mentions in order of who she liked most.

'The White Stripes were a bit better than Fatboy Slim, but not much.'

'Keane were nearly as good as Coldplay but neither was as good as Elvis Costello.'

'Although Echo and the Bunnymen are a big influence on Coldplay, Coldplay were far better. Echo and the Bunnymen were a lot better than the other 80s band New Order.'

'The Magic Numbers were the best. They were just fantastic.'

'Fat Boy Slim wasn't nearly as good as I thought he would be. It was definitely the worst show.'

1 *The Magic Numbers*   5 _____

2 _____   6 _____

3 _____   7 _____

4 _____   8 _____

b Complete the sentences with the words in the box.

| just | far | lot | nearly |
| nothing | better | ~~more~~ | a |

1 I find classical music much __more__ relaxing than any pop music.

2 Music these days is not _____ as imaginative as it was 20 years ago.

3 I think techno is a _____ more exciting than the dance music of the 1970s.

4 Country music is _____ as boring as folk music. I don't really like either.

5 The Beatles are _____ better than Oasis. I don't know how you can compare them.

6 Bands' images are _____ lot more important than their music these days. It's a shame.

7 Pop music is _____ like as good as jazz.

8 The live version of this song is even _____ than the studio version.

3 Pronunciation

✱ *record* (noun) vs. *record* (verb)

a ▶ CD4 T23 Listen and mark the stress on the words in italics.

1 We *export* a lot of coffee to Europe.

2 Sugar is our biggest *export*.

3 There's been an *increase* in car theft recently.

4 The graph shows that the number of university students *increases* every year.

5 I'm sorry. I didn't mean to *insult* you.

6 Don't do that with your hand. It's considered an *insult* here.

7 What a lovely *present*. Thank you.

8 We'd like to *present* you with the 'student of the month' certificate.

b ▶ CD4 T23 Listen again and repeat.

4 Vocabulary

✱ Listening to music

a What are the words? Complete the sentences.

1 I love dance music – anything with a good _beat_ (tabe) to it.

2 Most ＿＿＿＿＿ (scirly) these days are a bit silly but occasionally you get a songwriter with something to say.

3 Living in a small town, we don't get much ＿＿＿＿＿ (vile) music, a couple of shows a year if we're lucky.

4 It's a great ＿＿＿＿＿ (neut). It's so easy to sing along to.

5 I haven't got a great voice so I tend not to sing – I just ＿＿＿＿＿ (muh) along.

6 I used to work in a supermarket but that ＿＿＿＿＿ (kmauz) playing all day drove me crazy so I left.

7 We ＿＿＿＿＿ (decorred) our first CD in my dad's garage in three days.

8 ＿＿＿＿＿ (unranmtliest) music is great to play in the background when you're working.

b **Vocabulary bank** Complete the text with the words in the box. There are two you won't need.

| album   track   soundtrack   ~~label~~   canned music   cover   cover band   compose   singer-songwriter |

They say that a change is as good as a rest and this certainly seems true for Ricky Valentine. When he left Sony music two years ago to sign for a small independent record [1] _label_ , many people were predicting we'd heard the last from him. But this is not the case. His first [2] ＿＿＿＿＿ for Go-Go records is simply brilliant. *Back from the Dead* shows that Valentine is not just a great [3] ＿＿＿＿＿ (we all knew that anyway) but that he can [4] ＿＿＿＿＿ music on a much more ambitious level. This is not just a record of Valentine and his guitar. This is Valentine, his guitar and a full orchestra. At times you feel like you're listening to the [5] ＿＿＿＿＿ of some epic Hollywood production. It's quite amazing and quite unlike anything he's done before. The opening [6] ＿＿＿＿＿ which is a [7] ＿＿＿＿＿ of U2's *One* is mind-blowing. The rest of the songs (all original compositions) don't disappoint. If you only buy one CD this year, makes sure it's this one.

5 Grammar

✱ Embedded questions

a Complete the sentences with the correct question word, *who*, *when*, *why*, *where*, *what* or *how*.

1 I can't imagine _who_ told him.

2 I've forgotten ＿＿＿＿＿ her birthday is.

3 I wonder ＿＿＿＿＿ much it costs.

4 He didn't say ＿＿＿＿＿ he lives.

5 I don't know ＿＿＿＿＿ she didn't phone to say 'happy birthday'.

6 I don't understand ＿＿＿＿＿ she likes about him.

b Match the two parts of the sentences. Then add question marks or full stops.

1 It's easy to
2 Can you tell
3 Who told you
4 I'm thinking about where I want
5 Why didn't you
6 I don't know where
7 I don't understand
8 Do you

a how it works
b they went
c me why he did that
d come to my party
e know where he went
f to go on holiday this year
g see why he's so happy.
h where I live

6 Literature in mind

a Read this extract from *High Fidelity* by Nick Hornby. These statements are all true. Find evidence for each one in the text. There might be more than one thing for each statement.

1 Rob has been a DJ at the club before.
2 Rob doesn't think that Barry's band will be good.
3 Barry and his band are very good.
4 The people in the club are not teenagers.

Rob, the owner of the music store, is working one night as DJ in a nightclub. Barry, who works in Rob's store, has a band which is going to play in public for the first time at the club.

Before the band come on, everything's brilliant. It used to take a bit of time to warm people up, but tonight they're ¹ <u>up for it</u> straight away.

[And] I haven't lost any of the old magic. One sequence [of songs] has them begging for mercy. And then it's time for the band.

I've been told to introduce them; Barry has even written down what I'm supposed to say: 'Ladies and gentlemen, be afraid. Be very afraid. Here comes … SONIC DEATH MONKEY!' But […] in the end I just sort of mumble the name of the group into the microphone.

They're wearing suits and skinny ties, and when they plug in there's a terrible feedback ² <u>whine</u> which for a moment I fear is their opening number. But Sonic Death Monkey are no longer what they once were. They are no longer, in fact, Sonic Death Monkey.

'We're not called Sonic Death Monkey any more,' Barry says when he gets to the mike. 'We might be on the edge of becoming the Futuristics, but we haven't decided yet. Tonight, though, we're Backbeat. One two three … WELL SHAKE IT UP BABY …' And they launch into Twist and Shout, note perfect, and everyone in the place goes mad.

And Barry can sing.

They play Route 66 and Long Tall Sally and Money and Do You Love Me? and they ³ <u>encore</u> with In The Midnight Hour and La Bamba. Every song, in short, is ⁴ <u>naff</u> and recognizable, and guaranteed to please a crowd of thirtysomethings who think that hip-hop is something their children do in music and movement classes. The crowd are so pleased, in fact, that they ⁵ <u>sit out</u> the songs I have lined up for them to get them going again after Sonic Death Monkey have frightened and confused them.

'What was all that about?' I ask Barry when he comes up to the deck, sweaty and half-cut and pleased with himself.

'Was that all right?'

'It was better than what I was expecting.'

---

b (Circle) the words or phrases which are closest in meaning to the <u>underlined</u> words in the text.

1 a trying to leave   b enthusiastic   c cold
2 a an alcoholic drink   b an electric shock   c an unpleasant high sound
3 a play extra songs   b play badly   c play the same songs again
4 a unknown   b badly sung   c unfashionable
5 a don't like   b don't dance to   c go outside to sit down

c Read the text again and answer the questions.

1 What is 'the old magic' that Rob says he hasn't lost?
2 Why does Rob 'just sort of mumble the name of the group' when he introduces them?
3 What does the crowd think of the songs Rob plays when the band has finished?
4 What, in your opinion, does Rob feel about the evening at the club?

7 Write

a Read the concert review and underline the names of:

1 the two bands that played
2 two members of the main band
3 five songs that they played

CONCERTS – *Rolling Stones Special*

Fenway Park doesn't see many rock concerts. It's in a residential area and can't hold loud concerts late at night, for example. It seemed strange then, that the Rolling Stones chose this place in Boston to start the tour for their new CD, *A Bigger Bang*. **A** [ ] Indeed, council workers were there to measure sound levels. If the 'bang' was 'bigger' than 73 decibels, then it would have to be turned down.

Luckily, that wasn't necessary – although it might have been fun to see an official walk on stage to tell Keith Richards and the band to keep quiet. Imagine what the reaction would have been from the thousands of fans who had queued for hours to get into the stadium. Not nearly as polite as it was for The Black Eyed Peas, who played enthusiastic and energetic opening songs, I'm sure. But while the Peas did their best, it was clear who everyone was waiting for.

Just after eight, a huge roar erupted as the Stones began their show with *Start Me Up*. The crowd went wild. Five songs into the show and the band introduced *Rough Justice*, the first of several new tracks. I think this CD is going to be a huge hit. **B** [ ]

As the show continued with the band playing a mixture of old and new, I had to admire the energy of these men, who are all in their sixties now. Amazingly, they sound just as young and fresh as they did twenty years ago. Mick Jagger was quite amazing. **C** [1]

Then, while the band were playing *Miss You*, the huge stage opened up and a mini-stage came out taking the band into the heart of the audience. It was here that they played the best song of the night, *Satisfaction*. **D** [ ] Each song that Mick Jagger and the band played was accompanied by amazing special effects.

The lively *Jumping Jack Flash* made sure the show finished on a high note while the encores *You Can't Always Get What You Want* and *It's Only Rock 'n' Roll* sent the crowd home singing happily. This might have been the opening night but the band couldn't have sounded more professional. **E** [ ] It looks like the Stones are going to have a long and happy US tour.

b Read the text again and add the sentences. Write 1–6 in the boxes A–E. There is one sentence that you won't need.

1 No one knows better than him how to entertain.
2 The song would have taken the roof off the stadium, if it had had one.
3 Apparently they rehearsed for weeks for this tour and it showed.
4 Their music has taken the Stones all over the world.
5 They are, after all, a band that like to rock and roll as loud as possible.
6 And from their reaction, I think the crowd would agree with me.

c Write a review (200–250 words) of a show you've seen either live or on TV.

EXAM TIP

Justifying an opinion

- When you give an opinion in your writing, always write a supporting sentence to back it up. This will make your opinion sound more interesting.

- Look at Exercise 7b again. All the sentences that you added into the text support the writer's opinions. With these sentences, the text is more complete.

Unit check

1 Fill in the spaces

Complete the text with the words in the box.

> sensation   household   best   huge   which   name   ~~themselves~~   far   live   charts

The Arctic Monkeys confirmed [1] _themselves_ as an Indie music [2] _____ with the release of their
first CD, *Whatever people say I am, that's what I'm not*. It entered the album [3] _____ at number one
and became the [4] _____ -selling album of all time. The CD sold 360,000 copies, [5] _____ more
than Richard Ashcroft's second-placed *Keys to the World*. In a couple of months, the band from Sheffield
had gone from being almost unknown to being a [6] _____ name in the UK. The four boys started to
make a [7] _____ for themselves locally with their [8] _____ shows in 2003. People could then
get their songs for free on the internet, [9] _____ is how their popularity really grew. They then had
a couple of number one singles, *I bet you look good on the dance floor* and *When the sun goes down*,
but no one was quite expecting the [10] _____ success of their debut album.

| 9 |

2 Choose the correct answers

Circle the correct answer: a, b or c.

1   Do you know how _____ ?
    a old is she   b old her is   c (old she is)

2   Their new CD is _____ like as good as their first one.
    a nowhere   b not   c nothing

3   What an annoying tune! I just can't get it out of
    my _____ .
    a head   b mouth   c ears

4   Can you tell me what language _____ in Brazil?
    a they speak   b speak they   c do they speak

5   My dad thinks he's really cool singing _____ to my
    music. I think he's embarrassing.
    a on   b along   c out

6   Do you know what _____ ?
    a did he say   b he said   c said he

7   It's _____ as hot today as it was yesterday.
    a far   b just   c even

8   I didn't understand what _____ .
    a said he   b did he say   c he said

9   If you forget the words, just _____ along.
    a hum   b sing   c yawn

| 8 |

3 Vocabulary

Underline the correct word.

1   He's nowhere *far / close / near* as
    famous as his brother.

2   It's so embarrassing when my dad
    sings *along / though / on* to songs
    on the radio.

3   I love *alive / live / life* music. I go to
    at least two concerts a month.

4   I used to work in a shopping centre
    but the *tinned / frozen / canned*
    music they played all day drove me
    mad.

5   My brother's band has just signed to
    a big record *sign / label / brand*.

6   This CD is nothing *near / like / far*
    as good as their last CD.

7   The *words / tune / track* is easy to
    remember but the lyrics are difficult.

8   I'm in a band that mainly plays
    cover / copy / fake versions of
    famous songs.

9   I can't choose between them. I think
    they're *just / even / the same* as
    good as each other.

| 8 |

How did you do?

Total: | 25 |

| :) | Very good 20 – 25 | :\| | OK 14 – 19 | :(| Review Unit 11 again 0 – 13 |

12 Nature's best

1 Grammar

✳ Participle clauses

a Tick (✔) the correct sentences.

1 Watching the late-night film on TV, we fell asleep. ✔
2 Walking down the road, the sun was shining. ....
3 Sitting in a chair, the book was very interesting. ....
4 Having seen the film, I decided not to go to the cinema. ....
5 Having arrived two hours early, I had to wait in the airport. ....
6 Knowing no one there, the party was a bit boring. ....
7 Hearing a strange noise in the kitchen, I went to investigate. ....

b Rewrite the underlined sentences to make five new sentences using participle clauses.

◀ ▶ C ⌂   − ☐ ✕

¹I'm looking out over Guanabara Bay and I can't imagine anywhere else I'd rather be. The Sugar Loaf Mountain rises out of the sea at an impossible angle. You have to see it to believe it. ²The city of Rio de Janeiro hugs the hillsides behind me. It's one of the most beautiful places I've ever seen. Sand, sea and nightlife – I think I'm really going to enjoy this week of my South American adventure. We arrived here yesterday morning. ³We booked into a cheap hotel in the Gloria district and then made our way immediately to the beach. We lay there the whole day. ⁴Dave spent all day in the sun and then he spent all night complaining about sunburn. Of course, I was more sensible. ⁵I hired a deck-chair and an umbrella on the beach and spent most of the time reading my Rio de Janeiro guide. I found out that this whole area was discovered by the Portuguese, which is why Brazilians today don't speak Spanish like the rest of South America.

1 *Looking out over Guanabara Bay, I can't imagine anywhere else I'd rather be.*
2 ....
3 ....
4 ....
5 ....

2 Vocabulary

✱ Natural wonders

a Complete the sentences with the words in the box. There are three that you won't use.

> glacier   lake   cliffs   ~~coral reef~~   plain   desert   mountain range   bay   canyon

1   The Great Barrier _coral reef_ is off the coast of <u>Australia</u> / New Zealand.

2   _____ Titicaca is in Bolivia and Peru / Mexico and the USA.

3   The Grand _____ is in the USA / Mexico.

4   The Andes _____ is in South America / Europe.

5   The white _____ of Dover are on the coast of Ireland / England.

6   The Gobi _____ is in China / Japan.

b Now <u>underline</u> the correct country/countries to make the sentences true.

3 Grammar

✱ didn't need to / needn't have

a Which sentence matches each picture best? Write a or b. Choose *needn't have* where possible.

1  [a]

a   I didn't need to take a coat because it was a nice day.

b   I needn't have taken a coat because it was a nice day.

2

a   We needn't have arrived so early – there's no one here.

b   We didn't need to arrive so early – there's no one here.

3

a   You didn't need to take the stairs. The lift's working again.

b   You needn't have taken the stairs. The lift's working again.

4

a   I didn't need to wake up so early because it was Sunday.

b   I needn't have woken up so early because it was Sunday.

5

a   I didn't need to use the pay phone. I had my mobile.

b   I needn't have used the pay phone. I had my mobile.

6

a   He didn't need to run so fast. He won easily.

b   He needn't have run so fast. He won easily.

b Match the two parts of the sentences.

1   We didn't need to run

2   We needn't have run

3   We didn't need to eat at home

4   We needn't have eaten at home

5   We needn't have revised so hard

6   We didn't need to revise hard

a   because we knew there'd be food at the party.

b   because we already knew the subject so well.

c   because the test was so easy.

d   because there was food at the party.

e   because we had plenty of time to get to the station.

f   because the train was late anyway.

4 Vocabulary

✳ Travel verbs

a Complete the story with the prepositions in the box. You will use some more than once.

| for | on | to | back | out | away | off | in |

All I wanted was to get ¹ _____back_____ home. I had been ² _____ for two weeks, acting in a Chicken Shed Theatre show in London. Now I was tired, and I had a big bag of washing to do! Besides, a group of friends from school and I were all going ³ _____ holiday the next day. We were going ⁴ _____ the ferry to Amsterdam and we were all really excited. My parents had bought me a ticket so that I could fly home to Newcastle, to save time. I got ⁵ _____ the airport at 1 pm. My flight took ⁶ _____ at 3 pm, so I had plenty of time. When I got to the check-in, I learned my flight had been delayed an hour. An hour was no big deal, so I went ⁷ _____ a walk around the airport. When I got back I found out my flight had been cancelled altogether. In fact, all flights to Newcastle had been cancelled for the rest of the day. I couldn't waste a minute. I ran out of the airport and got ⁸ _____ a taxi. 'King's

Cross train station quickly, please!' I told the man. We set ⁹ _____ immediately. 'Good,' I thought. There was only one problem. The taxi driver was new to the job and got completely lost in central London. Three hours later I finally got ¹⁰ _____ of the taxi and ran into the station. I was in luck. There was a train leaving ¹¹ _____ Newcastle in ten minutes. It was the last one of the day and would get me there at 4 am. At least I would get home. I got ¹² _____ the train, found my seat, sat down and fell straight to sleep. The next thing I knew someone was talking to me loudly. I woke up with a jump. It was the train guard. 'Time to get ¹³ _____ the train, young lady,' he said. 'What?' I replied. 'Are we in Newcastle already?' 'Newcastle?' he said. 'We're in Edinburgh. We passed Newcastle an hour and a half ago.'

b ⬤ **Vocabulary bank** <u>Underline</u> the correct words.

1 We're going on a school _excursion_ / _expedition_ to Liverpool on Monday.

2 My mother's on a business _trip_ / _tour_ in Amsterdam until Friday.

3 Next year Mum and Dad are taking us on a five-week _tour_ / _trip_ round the US. I can't wait.

4 We're flying to Sydney with an overnight _excursion_ / _stopover_ in Singapore.

5 My grandma lives right in the north of Scotland. It's a ten-hour _trip_ / _journey_ to get there.

6 I have to _commute_ / _backpack_ two hours to work every day.

7 I'd hate to go on a _cruise_ / _journey_. Two weeks on a ship!? I'd go mad.

8 Their jungle _expedition_ / _voyage_ was a disaster and they had to return home after only three days.

5 Pronunciation

✳ /iː/ _seat_ and /ɪ/ _sit_

a ▶ **CD4 T24** Listen and (circle) the words you hear.

1 She _beat_ / (bit) her sandwich.

2 I'll _heat_ / _hit_ the chicken.

3 Can you _feel_ / _fill_ it?

4 The _sheep_ / _ship_ is leaving in the morning.

5 The _peach_ / _pitch_ was in bad condition.

6 Where did you put the _beans_ / _bins_?

7 Did he _leave_ / _live_ in the car?

8 Don't _sleep_ / _slip_!

b ▶ **CD4 T24** Listen again and repeat.

6 Read

a Read the text. Complete the sentences with one word in each space. There is often more than one possibility.

Over the last two hundred years, a lot of music has been [1] _written_ which tries to create, in sound, an emotionally charged picture of the natural world. Think of Vivaldi's *The Four Seasons* or Beethoven's *Pastoral Symphony*, to name only the [2] _____ famous.

One way in [3] _____ composers create these pictures is through imitating natural sounds. People have long recognised that humans are not the only creatures that make music. Birdsong is the most obvious [4] _____ of non-human music which composers have tried to recreate.

Perhaps the most bizarre musical collaboration [5] _____ humans and birds occurred in 1717, when *The Bird Fancyer's Delight* was published. This gave a selection of simple tunes which [6] _____ be played on a recorder to caged songbirds until the birds themselves learnt them off by [7] _____ – then you

could sit back and listen to your pet canary warble to the latest popular tune! However, if you wanted a bird to [8] _____ a more complex tune then, as *The Bird Fancyer's Delight* tells us, you had to spend hours playing music to it in a darkened room.

And it's not just birds, of course, that 'sing'. Recordings of whales 'singing' have been very popular in [9] _____ years. In China, some people keep caged cicadas [10] _____ of birds, because of the 'music' that they make!

Are the sounds made by animals just an expression of their feelings or instincts? Can we really [11] _____ them 'music'? Biologists tell us that a robin singing in a hedge is in fact claiming territory and warning other males to [12] _____ clear – hardly the equivalent of a song by Schubert, is it?

---

b ► **CD4 T25** Listen and complete the album titles.

1. Pacific _Blue_

2. *Coral* _____

3. *Classical* _____

4. **Eternal** _____

c ► **CD4 T25** Listen again and answer the questions.

Which CD ...

1 promises inspiration? _3_

2 features two very different musical instruments? _____

3 features two different types of water sounds? _____

4 mixes animal noises and human voices? _____

7 Listen

▶ **CD4 T26** Listen and complete the news report about holiday destinations and activities with a word or a number.

Beautiful Beaches

In our special beach survey we found that the beach is still the top holiday destination for American holiday-makers. Of the more than [1] _____1,000_____ people who answered our questionnaire, [2] _____% said they would 'definitely' or 'very likely' pay a visit to the beach sometime in the next year. And [3] _____% chose the beach as the perfect place for taking a holiday.

And what will they do when they get there? The top answer was have a party or a barbeque, while only 68% said they will get in the sea for a swim. Another 27% said they would get their [4] _____ wet, leaving 5% with no intention of getting in the water at all. Perhaps it's the thought of all those jellyfish, which just beat sharks as the nation's biggest fear about the sea.

Top five things to do on the beach

1	Have a party / barbeque	44%
2	Build a [5] _____	39%
3	Relax	32%
4	Hanging out with [6] _____	21%
5	Fly a kite	[7] _____%

Things to keep you out of the water

39% are concerned about jellyfish when getting in the sea – 2% more than those who are concerned about sharks.

5% of people who go to the beach do not get anywhere near the sea.

Most important qualities of a beach

1	Cleanliness	[8] _____%
2	View	46%
3	[9] _____	34%
4	Water temperature	23%

And the most popular beach in the nation is ...

Waikiki in [10] _____

LISTENING TIP

Filling in gaps to complete a text

- Read the question carefully, so you know what the topic is going to be.
- Find the blanks and look carefully at the words before and after them. Then guess what kind of information you will be listening out for. For example, is it a number, or the name of a country?

- Listen carefully for numbers. If you are very unsure, write the number which makes the most sense.
- Finally, it might sound obvious, but if the question asks you to fill in the gap with one word, then only use one word – not more.

Unit check

1 Fill in the spaces

Complete the text with the words in the box.

> beaches   islands   for   off   ~~Lying~~
> on   in   reefs   thunder   ever

¹ _Lying_ just off the coast of Lombok, the Gili ² _____ must be the most beautiful place I've ³ _____ seen. These three tiny islands were like jewels sparkling in the middle of the ocean. Beautiful white ⁴ _____ , clear blue sea and wonderful coral ⁵ _____ nearby for snorkelling. We went ⁶ _____ holiday there last year and had a great time. Getting there was quite an adventure, though. We left ⁷ _____ Indonesia from Heathrow late on a Sunday evening and arrived Monday afternoon in Bali in the middle of a huge ⁸ _____ storm. We got ⁹ _____ the plane and then we got ¹⁰ _____ a taxi to Lombok. This also involved getting on a ferry. Then we got on a boat to the Gili islands. After 36 hours' travelling, we finally arrived.

[9]

2 Choose the correct answers

(Circle) the correct answer: a, b or c.

1 They've gone _____ for a few days.
  a in   b out   c (away)

2 We must _____ now if we don't catch the train.
  a leave   b leaving   c to leave

3 We needn't have worried _____ the test was easy.
  a so   b because   c but

4 The _____ was surrounded by nothing but sea.
  a bay   b island   c lake

5 _____ on the beach, life couldn't get any better.
  a Read   b Reading   c To read

6 We were in the middle of a _____ , nothing but sand for miles around.
  a desert   b glacier   c bay

7 We arrived late because we set _____ later than we had planned.
  a for   b on   c off

8 I didn't need to get up early the next day, _____ I watched the late-night film.
  a because   b so   c but

9 My dad gets up early _____ breakfast for us.
  a make   b to make   c making

[8]

3 Vocabulary

Underline the correct words.

1 I'm just going on / _for_ / off a quick walk. I'll be back soon.

2 My daughter's going back_packing_ / -hiking / -camping around Europe for six months.

3 I'm not sure what time we'll get over / down / back, so don't wait up for us.

4 There were thousands of tiny fish swimming around the coral reef / plain / glacier.

5 It's a really long drive so I think we'll have to make a stop_over_ / -by / -in somewhere.

6 They've gone fishing at the desert / lake / canyon.

7 It will be the first manned voyage / tour / cruise to the moon for ten years.

8 We looked down from the top of the bay / cliff / canyon at the waves below us.

9 The band will be for / in / on tour until next April.

[8]

How did you do?

Total: [25]

|  Very good 20 – 25 | OK 14 – 19 |  Review Unit 12 again 0 – 13 |

1 Grammar

✱ Passive report structures

a Read the text and underline six examples of passive report structures.

How dolphins communicate

Bottle-nosed dolphins are known to be the most intelligent mammals after humans. One of the reasons for this is because of their amazing ability to 'speak' with each other. A large part of their brain is believed to be used for a communication system, which is very well developed in dolphins.

Although experts are not 100% sure, dolphins are also thought to have their own formal language. Each dolphin is believed to have his own whistle, almost as if it was their name.

Dolphins can't produce sounds in the same way as humans. They don't have vocal cords at the back of their necks, like we do.

Instead they use a complicated system of sounds such as whistles, squeaks, moans and clicks produced by the muscles in the blowhole, a small hole on the top of the dolphins' head. This sound system is known to be particularly useful at night or in dark waters as it also allows the dolphin to find his way even if he can't see very well. Dolphins are known to be able to produce sound frequencies from 0.25 to 200 kHz, with the lower frequencies used for communication.

b Read the newspaper extracts. Do the underlined parts of each sentence refer to the past or the present? Write _past_ or _present_.

1 The million-pound lottery winner is believed to live in the Manchester area. ___present___

2 Over fifty people are believed to have been killed by the storm. _____

3 The terrorists are thought to have entered the country last May. _____

4 The Queen is said to have been very happy about the news. _____

5 The man is known to be dangerous.

_____

6 The film, which is believed to have cost over $100 million, opens on Friday. _____

c Rewrite the following sentences using passive report structures.

1 Scientists think dinosaurs were wiped out by an ice age.

Dinosaurs are thought to have been wiped

out by an ice age. _____

2 People say this plant is good at helping you relax.

This plant _____

_____

3 Scientists think that elephants have good memories.

Elephants _____

_____

4 Experts believe this plant was used by our ancestors to cure headaches.

This plant _____

_____

5 Scientists say the last part of the forest was cut down more than 100 years ago.

The last part of the forest _____

_____

6 People know that some modern medicines actually do us harm.

Some modern medicines _____

_____

2 Vocabulary

✱ Health and medicine

a Find four words or phrases to do with health and medicine in the wordsnake.

operatingtheatrelocalanaestheticsurgeondiagnosis

1 _____ 2 _____ 3 _____ 4 _____

b Complete the dialogue with the words in the box.

symptoms   recovering   ~~doctor~~   diet   get better   check-up   suffer   diagnosed

Woman: Hello, you must be the new ¹ _doctor_ .

Doctor: Yes, I'm Doctor Lane. Are you here for a ² _____ ?

Woman: No, I haven't been feeling well recently.

Doctor: What are your ³ _____ ?

Woman: I often ⁴ _____ from headaches and I'm ⁵ _____ from the flu at the moment.

Doctor: Have you ever been ⁶ _____ with any serious illnesses?

Woman: No.

Doctor: Let me see. I think you may need some vitamins.

Woman: Will I need to change my ⁷ _____ ?

Doctor: No, just take these tablets and you should ⁸ _____ soon.

3 Pronunciation

✱ Consonant clusters

a ▶ CD4 T27 Match the words with the definitions. Listen and check.

1 A placebo
2 A scientist
3 A diagnosis
4 A symptom
5 A general anaesthetic

a is a doctor's opinion about a patient's illness.

b is a drug that makes you sleep during an operation so you do not feel anything.

c is a sign of illness in the body.

d is a substance with no active ingredients that is given to a patient.

e is someone who does research, usually in a laboratory.

b ▶ CD4 T27 Listen and repeat.

4 Vocabulary

✱ Feelings

a ▶ **CD4 T28** Listen to the conversation and match the two parts of the sentences. Write a–f in the boxes.

1	Katy's feeling sorry for herself	e	a	and it's making him exhausted.
2	Dilshan's over-anxious about work		b	and then she gets panicky.
3	Nick feels guilty		c	and it's getting her down.
4	Julia's got no confidence in herself		d	when he gets jealous.
5	My grandma's very nostalgic		e	because she's homesick.
6	Abby is absent-minded		f	and she always talks about when she was young.

b Read the text about emotional wellbeing. Some lines are correct and some have a word which should not be there. If a line is correct, put a tick (✔) in the space at the end of the line. If a word should not be there, cross it out and write the word in the space.

If you are feeling ~~it~~ anxious or depressed you may consider	1	*it*
keeping a thought diary. The first thing you should do is	2	✔
think about your problem and decide what can it is that is	3	_____
making you panicky or depressed. It's not important to work on	4	_____
out what that the cause is at this stage. The next step is to	5	_____
rate how very bad the problem is and pay attention to when it	6	_____
occurs. You may notice that a pattern. Now you need to	7	_____
decide what action you need to take and what behaviours you	8	_____
should to change first. Don't lose your confidence at this	9	_____
stage. It's easy to feel sorry for yourself and to think you'll	10	_____
never manage to change. Once you have decided on to your goals	11	_____
you need to work towards them at in your own time. Don't feel	12	_____
guilty if you are not going as fast as you hoped you would.	13	_____

c **Vocabulary bank** Replace the underlined words with a phrase from the box.

> on top of the world   ~~jealous~~   down   uneasy   over the moon   livid   irritable   uptight

1 My older brother thinks that Mum and Dad spoil me.
   He gets so <u>unhappy because I have what he wants</u>. *jealous*

2 I didn't do very well in the test, so I'm a bit <u>depressed</u> at the moment. _____

3 I don't think he really likes little children much, so I'm always a bit
   <u>worried and uncomfortable</u> when I take the kids to see him. _____

4 She said 'Yes.' She's going to marry me! I'm <u>extremely happy</u>. _____

5 Don't get <u>worried and nervous</u> . It's only a game of football. It's
   not the end of the world. _____

6 That's great news. I'm <u>very pleased</u> for you. _____

7 Kevin got into trouble at school. His mum was <u>extremely angry</u>
   when she found out. _____

8 Don't talk to dad today. He's very <u>easily annoyed</u>. _____

a Read the text quickly and find the names of seven diseases.

Sanitation

A few years ago *The British Medical Journal* launched a competition to decide the greatest medical breakthrough of all time. Fifteen 'discoveries' were put forward and the case for each was argued by prominent doctors from around the world. The shortlist included breakthroughs such as vaccines, the dangers of smoking, DNA and the use of computers. Members of the public were then invited to vote for which they felt was the most important. After more than 11,000 people had sent in their choices, the winner was finally announced. And with 1,975 votes the winner was ... sanitation.

Sanitation, which includes all aspects of delivering clean water to homes and taking the dirty water away, was championed by Professor Johan Mackenbach from University Medical Centre, Rotterdam, for the following reasons:

The Industrial Revolution was a time of great change. Before then, most people lived in the countryside and worked on the land. But the Industrial Revolution saw the opening of huge factories which led to the mass movement of people from rural living to towns. It also brought with it the need for sanitation.

At first the connection between crowded living conditions and illness went unrecognised, and infectious diseases were responsible for a great number of deaths. Tuberculosis, dysentery, diphtheria, typhoid, measles and smallpox were all common killers.

It was the cholera epidemic of the mid 19th century which started people thinking. John Snow, involved in the development of anaesthesia, was the one to show that shutting off a particular pump, in London's Broad Street, stopped the spread of cholera in the area.

But it was Edwin Chadwick, a lawyer, who came up with the idea of sewers and piped drinking water linked to people's houses to cut the risk of infection from poor urban drainage.

It took decades for his idea to be accepted. But it was, and between 1901 and 1970, deaths from diarrhoea and dysentery fell by around 12% in the UK.

In the 21st century, good sanitation is still a major problem in the developing world. Unsafe water, sanitation and hygiene were estimated to account for around 88% of the 1.8 million deaths from diarrhoeal disease in low and middle-income countries in 2001.

b Read the text again and answer the questions.

1 How was the winner of *The British Medical Journal*'s competition decided?

2 What is sanitation?

3 How did the Industrial Revolution change life in the UK?

4 How did crowded living conditions cause a rise in killer diseases?

5 What was John Snow's contribution to sanitation?

6 What was Edwin Chadwick's idea?

7 What were the results of a good sanitation system in the UK?

8 What evidence is there that poor sanitation remains a problem in much of the world?

Skills in mind

6 Read and write

Complete the dialogue with the correct words a, b, c or d.

Paula: Hi Joe, ¹ __how come__ you're so early?

Joe: I'm nervous ² _____ the computer exam.

Paula: Don't worry, you'll be fine.

Joe: No, I'm just ³ _____ the money for the exam. I'm not ready for it yet.

Paula: Don't say that, Joe. You're giving up before you try.

Joe: I can't see myself passing.

Paula: Well, Joe, if you want to pass, you need to change that. You need to see yourself passing.

Joe: ⁴ _____ than done.

Paula: ⁵ _____ a minute and listen to me!

Joe: OK, go ahead.

Paula: If you see yourself failing, you'll fail. If you see yourself passing, you'll pass.

Joe: I might as well try. I'll try ⁶ _____ at this stage.

Paula: If you think positive, you're ⁷ _____ to success!

1	a how long	b (how come)	c come on	d sort of
2	a of	b with	c about	d for
3	a throwing away	b throwing out	c throwing up	d throwing in
4	a Easy to	b Easier	c Better to say	d Easier said
5	a Hang in	b Hang out	c Hang up	d Hang on
6	a everything	b anything	c something	d nothing
7	a well on	b well done	c well on your way	d well down the way

EXAM TIP

Multiple-choice cloze

- Read the piece all the way through before you try to complete the sentences.

- Then read each sentence very carefully and try to understand what it will mean when the gap is filled.

- When you think you have found the correct answer, check that both the grammar and meaning are correct. If you are unsure, try saying the sentence to yourself with the other options in the gap. Do any of them sound right?

- Remember, you should always write something, even if you really don't know the answer. A sensible guess is better than no answer at all.

7 Study help

✶ Learning new words

When you learn new words and phrases in English, notice word combinations. Notice the difference between expressions such as *You're well* and *You're well on your way.* It's important to understand how words are used, not just their individual meanings. When you are reading a text, underline or highlight any unexpected or unusual combinations of words. See if you can work out the meaning from the context, then check it in a good dictionary. Fix the meaning by making sentences that are meaningful to you using that particular word combination.

Unit check

1 Fill in the spaces

Complete the text with the words in the box.

symptoms	is believed	taking	condition
was prescribed	specialised	~~diagnosed~~	
was performing	felt	medicine	

When Jonathan was a child he was ¹ _diagnosed_ with a rare skin problem. He ² _____ a strong medicine, which he had to take every day but as he grew older, his ³ _____ gradually got worse.

Then one evening he went to see a hypnotist who ⁴ _____ at the town hall. Jonathan was hypnotised at the front of the hall by the hypnotist. The next day he felt much better than usual. He even forgot to take his medicine but he ⁵ _____ fine. Jonathan told his doctor, who told him to see a medical hypnotist who ⁶ _____ in Jonathan's problem. That was three years ago. Jonathan has stopped ⁷ _____ most of his medicine and his ⁸ _____ have disappeared. Hypnotism ⁹ _____ by many doctors to be a powerful ¹⁰ _____ .

9

2 Choose the correct answers

Circle the correct answer: a, b or c.

1 Her car _____ in last week's crash.
   a is destroyed   b destroyed   c (was destroyed)

2 The new CD shop _____ to be excellent.
   a says   b is said   c saying

3 Children are often _____ to be faster language learners than adults.
   a said   b saying   c have said

4 She had her temperature _____ by the nurse.
   a taken   b done   c made

5 When was your last _____ at the doctor's?
   a check-up   b check-in   c check out

6 I _____ from car sickness since I was a child.
   a was suffering   b have suffered   c am suffering

7 He's known to _____ of cholera.
   a be dead   b die   c have died

8 Five per cent of the population of Britain are _____ with depression every year.
   a suffered   b operated   c diagnosed

9 It is _____ by some scientists that humans developed from dolphins.
   a thought   b have thought   c thinking

8

3 Vocabulary

Rewrite the sentences using the word in brackets.

1 He tends to get very worried, very quickly. (panicky)
   He's very panicky.

2 We were so happy when we heard the news. (moon)
   _____

3 I couldn't be happier. (world)
   _____

4 Don't worry so much. (anxious)
   _____

5 He got better really quickly. (recovery)
   _____

6 She had a really bad headache. (suffering)
   _____

7 He forgets everything I tell him. (minded)
   _____

8 The doctor wants to cut the tumour out. (operate)
   _____

9 I went to the doctor to make sure everything is OK. (check-up)
   _____

8

How did you do?

Total: **25**

  Very good 20 – 25   OK 14 – 19    Review Unit 13 again 0 – 13

14 Movie magic

1 Grammar

✱ Clauses of purpose: *to / in order to / so as to*

a Match the two parts of the sentences.

1 I got up at 5 am in order to
2 Dad took the car to the mechanic to
3 The kidnappers gave them an extra week so as to
4 The government kept it a secret in order not to
5 Mum told us to turn the music down in order not to
6 We booked a hotel online so as not to

a give them the chance to raise the money.
b take some photos of the sunrise.
c create a public panic.
d waste time looking for one when we got there.
e get the brakes checked.
f wake up Dad.

b Choose the correct words to complete the story.

X-Men IV was going to be the biggest film of the year. I had to be there at the cinema on the day that it opened [1] *so as not to / so as to* lose my status of being the world's biggest X-Man fan.

I bought my ticket two weeks before on the internet [2] *so as not to / so as to* make sure I'd get one. I didn't want to arrive at the cinema and find they'd sold out. I got a ticket right at the front [3] *in order not to / in order to* run the risk of a big tall man sitting in front of me and blocking the screen.

On the day, I left home at 1 pm [4] *in order not to / in order to* arrive at the cinema early and avoid the queue. I stopped on the way at the newsagent's [5] *not to / to* buy crisps, sweets and cola. I bought loads [6] *so as not to / so as to* have to leave the film in the middle if I got hungry.

I got to the cinema and found my seat. I turned off my mobile phone [7] *in order not to / in order to* be disturbed and because a big advert on the screen told me to. Then the film started and I sat back in my seat [8] *not to / to* enjoy the film. It was only then that I realised I'd left my glasses at home.

c Join the two sentences to make one. Use the word in **bold** at the end.

1 I got up at 6 am. I wanted to drive my friend to the airport. **(to)**
   I got up at 6 am to drive my friend to the airport.

2 We got to the stadium early. We didn't want to miss the start of the game. **(in order not to)**

3 I phoned Michelle. I wanted to invite her to my party. **(so as to)**

4 I didn't tell Ahmed about the accident. I didn't want to worry him. **(so as not to)**

5 I took the train. I didn't want to get caught in a traffic jam. **(in order not to)**

6 I'd like to speak to her. I want to apologise. **(so as to)**

7 He's saving all his money. He wants to buy a new computer. **(to)**

8 Can you speak quietly? You are disturbing other people. **(so as not to)**

2 Grammar

✷ Result clauses with
so / such (that)

a Underline the correct option.

1 We've lived here *so* / *such* long that we don't even notice the planes any more.

2 It was *so* / *such* an easy test that everyone passed.

3 It was *so* / *such* dark that we couldn't see a thing.

4 I've eaten *so* / *such* much food I could explode.

5 He was *so* / *such* tired that he just wanted to go to bed.

6 It was *so* / *such* a long film that most people fell asleep before the end.

b Complete the sentences with *so* or *such*.

1 I've got ___*such*___ a bad memory that things just slip my mind all the time.

2 I'm _____ scared of pain that I always ask the dentist to give me an injection.

3 She spends _____ much time on the phone that I never get a chance to use it.

4 Dave's _____ a witty man that I can't help laughing whenever I'm with him.

5 She went to _____ great lengths to arrange this party for you, you should at least say 'thank you'.

6 They've fallen out _____ badly that I don't think they'll ever make up again this time.

7 We've got _____ many signatures on our petition that they'll have to take notice.

8 I'm _____ tired that I can't stop yawning.

c Join the two sentences to make one. Use *so / such ... that.*

1 I'm really tired. I'm going to bed early tonight.

   I'm so tired that I'm going to bed early tonight.

2 Nigel's really careless. He breaks something every time he comes to my house.

   ----

3 We set out very late. We didn't arrive until midnight.

   ----

4 That's a nasty cough. You should see a doctor.

   ----

5 United played badly. They were beaten 5–1.

   ----

6 Rob's a really intellectual person. It's difficult to understand everything he talks about.

   ----

7 The sponsored walk was a great success. We're going to organise another one.

   ----

8 He snored really loudly. I couldn't get to sleep.

   ----

3 Pronunciation

✷ Word stress in multi-syllabic words

a ▶ CD4 T29 Listen and mark the stress on each word.

1 million
2 millionaire
3 confront
4 confrontation
5 problem
6 problematic
7 adapt
8 adaptation
9 recommend
10 recommendation

b ▶ CD4 T29 Listen again and repeat.

4 Vocabulary

✳ Reacting to films

a Read the sentences and write the numbers 1–8 in the correct boxes.

1 Jessica jumped out of her seat.
2 Frank fell about laughing.
3 Yves couldn't stop yawning.
4 Charlie chuckled.
5 Carol cried her eyes out.
6 Erika was on the edge of her seat.
7 Sara screamed.
8 Brian bit his lip.

b What real films do you think each of these people might be watching? Give your reasons.

1 Jessica might be watching
   Scream III because it's a very scary film.
2 Frank might be watching _____
   _____ .
3 Yves might be watching _____ .
4 Charlie might be watching _____ .
5 Carol might be watching _____ .
6 Erika might be watching _____ .
7 Sara might be watching _____ .
8 Brian might be watching _____ .

c Complete the sentences with the words in the box.

> laughing   crying   sitting   screaming   jumping   chuckling   ~~yawning~~   biting

1 The lesson was so boring that I couldn't stop _yawning_ .
2 We fell about _____ . I don't think I've ever seen anything quite so funny.
3 You could hardly hear the band play because there were so many teenage girls _____ .
4 We spent the whole game _____ on the edge of our seats, it was so exciting.
5 Why are you _____ to yourself? What's so funny?
6 I spent the whole film _____ my lip. I was determined not to cry.
7 My dad spent the whole wedding _____ his eyes out.
8 The film had us _____ out of our seats every five minutes.

d **Vocabulary bank** Complete the sentences with the words in the box.

> lip   nails   face   ~~goose~~
> joy   hands   hair   laugh

1 I get _goose_-bumps just thinking about talking to her.
2 I know you're nervous but try not to bite your _____ .
3 He won't listen to anything I say. He makes me want to pull my _____ out.
4 Mum cried for _____ when I told her she was going to be a grandmother soon.
5 When my dad asked Tom if he was my boyfriend I just hid my _____ in my hands.
6 The film was so funny it made me _____ out loud.
7 Dad threw his _____ up in horror when I told him I'd crashed his car.
8 As I sat there waiting for the exam to begin, I started chewing my _____ .

5 Everyday English

a Put the words in order to make expressions.

a   easy / I'm   *I'm easy.*

b   the / tongue / of / tip / it's / on / my

c   rings / that / bell / a

d   and / that / this

e   mind / in / got / anything ?

f   way / the / it / through / all

b Read the dialogue. Replace the underlined phrases with the expressions in Exercise 5a. Write a–f in the boxes.

Ana: Hey, Paula. What have you got planned this weekend?

Paula: [1] A few different things. Nothing special, though. Why? ☐

Ana: Do you want to do something this evening?

Paula: Sure. Why not? [2] Have you already made any plans? ☐

Ana: Not really. [3] I'm open to suggestions. What about you? ☐

Paula: Well, I wouldn't mind going to the cinema.

Ana: That's a great idea. What's on?

Paula: There's that new film with erm.. Oh what's his name? [4] I can't quite remember it. You know... ☐

Ana: No, I don't. Who?

Paula: That one who was in all those films about kids singing at school.

Ana: Do you mean *High School Musical*?

Paula: [5] That sounds familiar. Yeah. That's the film. Who was in that? ☐

Ana: Only my favourite actor, Zak Efron.

Paula: Yeah. That's him. I wouldn't mind seeing his new film.

Ana: I've already seen it five times.

Paula: So I don't suppose you'd want to watch [6] it from the beginning to the end again? ☐

Ana: Of course I would! I love him.

6 Study help

✳ Checking your writing

It's not always easy to spot the mistakes in your own writing. Ideally, you should get someone else to have a look and help you if you can. If this isn't possible, try to follow these guidelines:

● As soon as you finish, quickly read through and correct any obvious mistakes you see. Do not try to do a complete check now. Often you will only see exactly what you think you have written.

● Wait for a while (a day or two if you have time) and return to your writing with fresh eyes. Read through your work at a normal speed. This is just to remind you of what you have written and for you to get an overall impression of your work. Do not correct anything at this stage.

● Now read it again more carefully. Take each sentence one at a time and read it to yourself slowly. Read exactly what you see on the page – not what you think should be there. Make corrections.

● Read through one last time. It's a good idea to do this out loud if possible, because then you can hear if it sounds natural and reads easily.

● If you have any questions about the organisation of the writing, or the grammar or vocabulary, ask your teacher if you can write these questions at the bottom of your writing. Then your teacher can answer them.

Now your writing should be ready to hand in.

7 Read

a Read through the DVD recommendations and for each one, <u>underline</u> the names of the director and the leading actors.

b Read the texts again. Put phrases 1–6 into the correct places.

1 to stop being part of the programme
2 has no idea about how he is exploited
3 to save a failing TV station
4 to stay in the real world forever
5 to take a break from everyday life
6 to be seen by millions of viewers

READING TIP

Putting parts of a text into the correct place

- Make sure you read all the text first.
- Read again before (and after, if appropriate) each space. Read carefully and look for clues about what might go in the space.
- Sometimes there might be grammatical clues to help. In exercise 7b, for example, number 2 can only fit, grammatically, into space D.
- Usually though, you will need to pay close attention to meaning more than anything else. For example, number 1 refers to 'the programme' so look for a piece of text which has already referred to 'a programme', and then you are more likely to find the correct place for the phrase.

DVD Decisions – looking for a good film to rent? Let us help you.

Fiction or Reality?

Here are some recommendations for classic films to watch this weekend – each of them explores the themes of cinema, fiction and reality.

The Purple Rose of Cairo (1985)

One reason to go to the movies is
A _____ and lose yourself in the magic of the silver screen. In *The Purple Rose of Cairo*, Woody Allen turns this idea on its head.

   Mia Farrow plays Cecilia, a New Jersey waitress looking for escape from her boring life in the local cinema. Jeff Daniels is Tom Baxter, the handsome archaeologist hero in a film called *The Purple Rose of Cairo*, which Cecilia has already seen several times. One day Baxter decides he's had enough of being a character in a film, and he walks out of the screen to join Cecilia in the cinema. Can Hollywood find Tom and get him back into the film or will he manage B _____ ?

EDtv (1999)

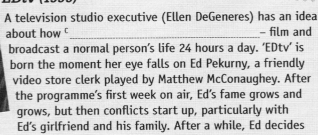

A television studio executive (Ellen DeGeneres) has an idea about how C _____ – film and broadcast a normal person's life 24 hours a day. 'EDtv' is born the moment her eye falls on Ed Pekurny, a friendly video store clerk played by Matthew McConaughey. After the programme's first week on air, Ed's fame grows and grows, but then conflicts start up, particularly with Ed's girlfriend and his family. After a while, Ed decides he wants D _____ , but he finds out his contract can't be reversed. But in a country that switches the TV set on at breakfast and off at bedtime, anything can happen... Ron Howard's comedy is well worth watching.

The Truman Show (1998)

As a movie fan, do you also enjoy TV reality shows?

   In reality shows, people choose
E _____
– but what if they didn't even know they were in a show? Peter Weir's *The Truman Show* takes this idea and plays with it wonderfully.

   Jim Carrey is Truman, a man whose life is fake. His home town is really a huge studio with hidden cameras everywhere, and all his friends and the people around him (even his wife, played by Laura Linney) are actors in the most popular TV series in the world: *The Truman Show*, directed by Christof (the actor Ed Harris), the man who actually runs Truman's life. Truman believes he is an ordinary man with an ordinary life and F _____ – until one day, he finds out everything. His attempt to break away and start his own, unwatched life is moving and thought-provoking.

Unit check

1 Fill in the spaces

Complete the text with the words in the box.

a	such	chuckled	order	should
so	~~comedy~~	which	about	not

The last film I saw was a ¹ _comedy_ called *The Pink Panther*. It's about a detective called Inspector Clouseau. He is called in by the French police in ² _____ to solve a diamond robbery. The only problem is that Clouseau has ³ _____ many accidents that whatever he does always ends in disaster. It stars Steve Martin who is such ⁴ _____ good actor that I fell ⁵ _____ laughing every time he walked onto the screen. It was ⁶ _____ a funny film! I won't say any more so as ⁷ _____ to give the ending away, ⁸ _____ is brilliant, by the way. I went with my dad. He only ⁹ _____ to himself a few times. He told me that I ¹⁰ _____ see the original from the 1960s with an actor called Peter Sellers.

[ ] **9**

2 Choose the correct answers

(Circle) the correct answer: a, b or c.

1 I didn't want to cry so I bit my _____ .
   a mouth   b cheek   c (lip)

2 I spoke to the manager _____ complain.
   a for to   b so as   c in order to

3 It was _____ a hot day that I felt ill.
   a so   b such   c really

4 The game was so exciting that we were on the _____ of our seats for ninety minutes.
   a side   b top   c edge

5 I phoned him _____ invite him to my party.
   a to   b for   c so

6 He must have said something funny because everyone fell _____ laughing.
   a about   b over   c out

7 We're _____ happy that we're going out tonight to celebrate.
   a too   b so   c such

8 The film was so sad that I cried my eyes _____ .
   a over   b out   c up

9 We set off really early _____ as not to get stuck in the traffic.
   a for   b to   c so

[ ] **8**

3 Vocabulary

What are the words? Complete the sentences.

1 When he told us what happened, we all just lefl _fell_ about laughing.
2 I was so nervous I started giitbn _____ my lip.
3 I'm so cold, I've got sogoe-pubms _____ .
4 The book wasn't hilarious but I did find myself lucihkncg _____ a few times.
5 If you can't stop wanngiy _____ you should go to bed.
6 She threw her hands up in rrroho _____ when she saw the mess we had made in the living room.
7 When the monster made its first appearance I pejmud _____ out of my seat.
8 I know it's a bad habit but I can't help biting my slain _____ , especially when I'm nervous.
9 When the actors got out of the limousine, all their fans started grimacens _____ .

[ ] **8**

How did you do?

Total: [25]

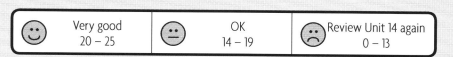

| 😃 Very good 20 – 25 | 😐 OK 14 – 19 | 🙁 Review Unit 14 again 0 – 13 |

Grammar reference

Unit 1

Relative clauses: review

1 We use relative clauses to add information about the subject or object of a sentence.

2 Relative clauses are introduced with words like *who, that, which, where* and *whose*.
We use *who* or *that* to refer to people.
*He's the man **who / that** wrote the article.*
We use *which* or *that* to refer to things.
*The newspaper **which / that** gives the best news is* The Daily Standard.
We use *where* to refer to places.
*That's the building **where** my sister works.*
We use *whose* to refer to possession.
*She's the woman **whose** house got destroyed in the flood.*

3 A defining relative clause gives essential information about the thing or person we are talking about. In this case we do not use a comma.
*The man **who** works in this office is very intelligent.*
(= I am talking about the only man who works in this office.)

4 A non-defining relative clause gives information that is simply additional about the thing or person we are talking about. The extra information is between commas.
*The man, **who** works in this office, is very intelligent.*
(= I am talking about an intelligent man and adding the non-essential information that he works in this office.)

Unit 2

what clauses

1 The word *what* can be used to mean *the thing that*, and can be used as the subject or object of a verb.
***What** (the thing that) makes me angry is the way he talks to people.* (subject)
*I can't remember **what** (the thing that) he said.* (object)

2 When *what* begins the sentence, we can use words like *that / why / when* (etc.) to join the second part of the sentence.
***What** you don't understand is **that** people are all different.*
***What** I don't like is **when** people want me to be the same as them.*

Verbs + gerund/infinitive review

Some verbs (*remember, stop, try*) can be followed by a second verb in either the gerund form or the infinitive form. The form of the second verb depends on the meaning of the sentence.

Remember
*I **remember phoning** her to invite her. (= I phoned, and I remember that I did that.)*
*I **remembered to phone** her and invite her. (= I nearly forgot to phone, but I remembered and then I phoned.)*

Stop
*The teacher **stopped talking** and left the room. (= The teacher was talking, then she stopped and left the room.)*
*When I was walking down the street, I **stopped to talk** to a friend of mine. (= I stopped walking, and after I stopped I began to talk to a friend.)*

Try
*I **tried closing** the door but I could still hear the noise. (= It was noisy outside. I closed the door. When the door was closed, I could still hear the noise outside.)*
*I **tried to close** the door but it was stuck. (= I wanted to close the door, and I tried, but I was unsuccessful.)*

Unit 3

Reported speech

1 When we report what someone said, there is often a change in verb tense between the direct speech (the person's actual words) and the indirect (reported) speech. The verb goes 'one step back':

I'm tired,' he said yesterday.	→	*He said yesterday that he **was** tired.*
*'Someone's **stolen** my bicycle!' he said.*	→	*He said someone **had stolen** his bicycle.*
*'I **can't** lift this,' she said.*	→	*She said that she **couldn't** lift it.*

2 We do not necessarily change the verb tense if the information in the direct speech is still true.

'He's Italian,' she told me.	→	*She told me that he's Italian.*
*'I **was** born in London,' Amanda said.*	→	*Amanda said that she **was** born in London.*

Reporting verbs

We can use many different verbs to report speech. Note that the patterns that follow the verbs are different.

1 Some verbs (e.g. *say / claim / state / emphasise*) are followed by *that* + clause.
*He **emphasised that** the work was very important.*
*The prime minister **claimed that** the economy had improved.*

2 Some verbs (e.g. *promise / refuse*) are followed by the infinitive with *to*.
*She **promised to help** me in the evening.*
*My father **refused to let** me stay out late.*
Note that we can also use *promise* with the structure *promise* + person + *that*.
*She **promised me that I could** take her to the cinema.*

3 Some verbs (e.g. *encourage / advise / persuade*) are followed by an object (person) + the infinitive with *to*.
*He **advised me to relax** sometimes.*
*I **persuaded them to come** with me.*

4 Some verbs (e.g. *recommend / suggest / deny*) are followed by a noun or gerund.
*I recommended **the new Green Day CD / listening** to the new Green Day CD.*
*They suggested **the French restaurant / eating** at the French restaurant.*

Unit 4

used to and *would*

1 We can use the expression *used to* + verb to talk about habits and customs in the past (things that are no longer true).
*My father **used to smoke**. (= My father smoked in the past but he doesn't any more.)*
*When I was young, I **used to go** swimming every day. (= That was my habit but I don't do this any more.)*

2 It is also possible to use *would* + verb to talk about habits and customs in the past.
*My mother **would cook** chicken every Sunday. (= This was a custom of my mother's.)*
*At school, I **would** always **ask** the teacher questions. (= This was a habit of mine when I was a schoolchild.)*

3 The difference between *used to* and *would* is that we can only use *would* for repeated actions – we cannot use it for a permanent state or situation.
*We **used to live** in London. (A permanent state or situation: We would live in London is not possible.)*
*I used to visit my grandparents every weekend. (A repeated action: I **would visit** my grandparents every weekend is possible.)*

Adverbial phrases

1 We use adverbs to describe verbs — often to say how an action is/was performed.
*They played **well**.*
*Drive more **slowly**!*
*He reacted **angrily** to what I said.*

2 We can also use phrases to describe a verb and to say how an action is/was performed. These phrases are called **adverbial phrases** because they are like adverbs but are more than one word.

3 One structure for adverbial phrases is *with* + noun.
*My brother looked at me **with surprise**.*
*I finished my homework **with difficulty**.*
*I listened to the programme **with great interest**.*

4 Another structure for adverbial phrases is *in a(n)* + adjective + *way*.
   *They asked me lots of questions, but **in a friendly way**.*
   *We worked hard, but **in a fun way**.*
   *I like listening to her because she talks **in an interesting way**.*

   Adverbial phrases are often used when an adjective (e.g. *friendly, difficult, interesting, fun*) has no adverb form.

Unit 5

Conditionals

1 We use the **zero conditional** to talk about a condition and consequence that are always true.
   *If you **don't eat**, you **die**.*

2 We use the **first conditional** to talk about a possible present situation and its possible future consequence.
   *If we **raise** enough money, we'**ll build** a hospital.*

3 We use the **second conditional** to talk about a hypothetical situation in the present and its future consequence, which may be very unlikely or impossible.
   *If I **was** prime minister, I'**d increase** the money we spend on helping other countries.*

4 We use the **third conditional** to talk about a hypothetical situation and consequence in the past which is, therefore, impossible to change.
   *If the food **had got** there quicker, we'**d have** saved thousands of lives.*

Mixed conditionals

Conditional sentences do not always follow the four patterns described above. For example, it is common to find mixtures of second and third conditionals.

1 If we want to talk about a past action and its present consequence, then the *if* clause follows the pattern of a third conditional and the consequence clause follows the pattern of a second conditional.
   *If more people **had signed** the petition, the shopping centre **wouldn't be** here. (= Not many people signed the petition, so the shopping centre is here.)*
   *If I **hadn't missed** the plane, I'**d be** in Egypt now. (= I missed the plane. I'm not in Egypt.)*

2 If we want to talk about how a universal truth affected a past action, then the *if* clause follows the pattern of a second conditional and the consequence clause follows the pattern of a third conditional.
   *If the world **was** a fairer place, those people **wouldn't have died**. (= The people died because the world is not a fair place.)*
   *If I **spoke** Indonesian, I **would have understood** what he said. (= I didn't understand what he said because I don't speak Indonesian.)*

Unit 6

Future continuous

1 If we want to talk about an action that will be in progress at a specified future time, we use the future continuous tense.
   ***Twenty years from now** people **will be living** under the sea.*
   ***Later this month** I'**ll be visiting** a project in the Sudan.*

2 The future continuous is formed by *will* + *be* + the *-ing* form of the verb.

Future perfect

1 If we want to talk about an action that will have been completed by a specified future time, we use the future perfect tense.
   ***By 2050** ninety per cent of the Amazon **will have vanished**.*
   ***By the time the World Cup finishes**, I'**ll have watched** more than 60 hours of football.*

2 The future perfect tense is formed by *will* + the present perfect.

Future time expressions

There are a number of words we can use to show that we are talking about a future time, e.g. *during, for, by, until, XXX from now* and *in XXX's time*.

1 *XXX from now* and *in XXX's time* both refer to a specific time in the future.
   ***Twenty years from now**, no one will be using petrol cars.*
   *The film starts **in ten minutes' time**.*

2 *During* is used to refer to a period of future time when something will happen.
   *Scientists will be working on a solution **during** the next three years.*

3 *For* refers to how long a future event will last.
   *They'll be studying climate change **for** the next five years.*

4 *By* refers to a future deadline – the action will be completed before this time.
   *I'll have finished my report **by** Thursday. (= some time between now and Thursday.)*

5 *Until* also refers to a future deadline. It emphasises that a continuous action will stop at the specified time.
   *We'll be working **until** three. (= We will stop working at three.)*

Unit 7

Past perfect passive

1 We use the past perfect to make it very clear that a past action happened <u>before</u> another action.
   *When we got to the party, James **had left**.*

2 We use the past perfect passive to say that a past action happened before another one, but also when we do not know who did the action, or that it is not important who did it.
   *I got to the shop late, and all the ice cream **had been sold**.*
   *I was surprised to find this old book – I thought it **had been thrown** away.*
   *My home town looked different because several new shops **had been built**.*

3 The past perfect passive is formed with the past perfect of the verb *to be* (*had (not) been*) + the past participle of the main verb.

Past perfect continuous

1 We use the past perfect continuous to talk about ongoing actions that began before another action in the past.
   *When I got to the party, my friends **had been dancing** for more than an hour.*
   *Her eyes were red, so he knew that she **had been crying**.*
   *When my mother called me for dinner, I **had been reading** for two hours.*

2 The past perfect continuous is formed with the past perfect of the verb *to be* (*had (not) been*) + the *-ing* form of the main verb.

Unit 8

Dummy *it*

1 We often use the word *it* to introduce sentences in English, and often it does not refer to an actual thing. For example, we use *it* when we say hello:
   ***It's** nice to meet you.*

2 The structure is often *It + be +* adjective + infinitive with *to*.
   ***It's interesting to listen to** her ideas.*
   ***It's wonderful to see** people smile.*
   ***It's important to understand** this point.*

3 The structure can also be *It +* verb + *to* infinitive.
   ***It hurts to see** people cry.*
   ***It feels great to be back** in the town where I was born.*

Modals review

1 Modal verbs say how the speaker or writer views a situation or action, in the present, the past or the future. They are used to say something about certainty, possibility, or whether something is necessary, permitted or forbidden.
   *I **might** see you tomorrow. (possible)*
   *I **will** see him tomorrow. (certain)*
   *You **must** come and see us. (necessary)*
   *You **can't** come in here. (forbidden)*

2 We use modal verbs to express a wide range of functions.
   *I think it **will** rain tonight. (prediction)*
   ***May** I come in? (asking for permission)*
   *They **might not** arrive on time. (possibility)*
   *You **mustn't** do that. (prohibition)*
   *She **can** run a marathon in three hours. (ability)*

*I **must** remember to buy some stamps.* (obligation)
*They **must have been** tired at the end of the race.* (deduction, past)
*You **could** phone Peter and ask him.* (suggestion)

3   All modal verbs are followed by the infinitive without *to*. They are auxiliaries and do not need (e.g.) *do/does/did* to make negatives and questions.

Unit 9

Phrasal verbs

These points may help you remember how to use phrasal verbs correctly.

1   Can the phrasal verb be split?

There is no problem here if the verb is intransitive (this means that the verb doesn't take an object) because there is no object.
*We find it hard to **get by** on just one salary.* (There is no object to split *get* and *by*.)

2   If the verb is transitive, we need to know if the verb is separable or not. If it is not separable, then the two parts need to keep together.
*The report **looks into** problems facing workers in poor countries.*
NOT: ~~The report **looks** problems facing workers in poor countries **into**.~~

Note how the *Cambridge Advanced Learner's Dictionary* identifies this kind of verb: *look into **sth***

3   With separable phrasal verbs, the object can come between the two parts.
*We **looked** his name **up** on the internet.*
*We **looked up** his name on the internet.*

Note how the *Cambridge Advanced Learner's Dictionary* identifies this kind of verb: *look **sth** up*

4   If we use a pronoun with a separable phrasal verb, then it must come between the two parts.
*I don't believe you. You **made** it **up**.*
NOT: ~~I don't believe you. You **made up** it.~~

5   Finally, some phrasal verbs have three (or more) parts. These cannot be split.
*The big companies **get away with** murder.*
*I don't know why people **put up with** it.*

Unit 10

Reduced relative clauses

When a relative clause is passive, we can leave out the relative pronoun and the verb *to be*.
*The shopping centre, **(that was)** opened by the Queen, is the biggest in the country.*
*The book **(that was)** written by Madonna has become a huge success.*

Question tags review

1   Question tags are commonly used in conversation to confirm what we think is true.
*You're interested in politics, **aren't you**? (= If I remember correctly, you're interested in politics.)*

2   We also use question tags to make conversation.
*Young people should show more interest in politics, **shouldn't they**? (= This is not a question but what I believe.)*

3   When the main clause is positive, the tag is negative.
*Footballers **get** paid too much, **don't they**?*
*You **will** come to my party, **won't you**?*

4   Similarly, if the main clause is negative, the tag is positive.
*Pop stars like Bono **can't** make a real difference, **can they**?*
*You **don't** live around here, **do you**?*

Unit 11

Indirect questions

1 We often use indirect questions to ask people for information. They are considered more polite. Indirect questions often start with expressions like *Can you tell me ... Do you know ...* and *Could I ask you ...*

2 When we use indirect questions, the word order that follows the question word is that of a statement and <u>not</u> a question.
*Can you tell me **when the film starts**?* (NOT: ~~Can you tell me when does the film start?~~)
*Could I ask you **where you got my name from**?* (NOT: ~~Could I ask you where did you get my name from?~~)
*Do you know **why she said that**?* (NOT: ~~Do you know why did she say that?~~)

3 If we are expecting a yes/no answer, we use *if* or *whether*.
*Can you tell me **if** the film has started yet?*
*Do you know **whether** she still lives there?*

Embedded questions

Words such as *who, when, where* and *why* are not always used to ask questions. They are often found as part of a statement. In these cases they are not followed by the question word order.
*I can't remember **where I heard** that song before.*
(NOT: ~~I can't remember where did I hear that song before.~~)
*I don't know **why you like** that song – it's terrible.* (NOT: ~~I don't know why do you like that song.~~)
*I want to know **who he is**.* (NOT: ~~I want to know who is he.~~)

Unit 12

Participle clauses

In participle clauses, we use the *-ing* form of the verb to combine two clauses that share the same subject. They can be used:

1 to talk about two events that happen(ed) at the same time.
***Looking out** across the sea, I couldn't imagine a more beautiful view. (= At the same time as looking out across the sea, I was also thinking about how beautiful the view was.)*
***Drinking** a cool lemonade, he stretched out on the sand. (= At the same time as stretching out on the sand he was drinking a lemonade.)*

2 to talk about an action that happened before the other action in the sentence.
***Having paid** the bill, we left the hotel. (= We paid the bill and then left the hotel.)*
***Having written** the postcard, I looked for a post office to buy a stamp. (= I wrote the postcard and then looked for a post office.)*
NB in this case we use *having* followed by the past participle.

3 Remember, the subject of both clauses must be the same.
~~Looking up in the sky, the moon was beautiful.~~
This suggests the moon was looking up into the sky, which does not make sense.
Looking up in the sky, I noticed how beautiful the moon was.
This sentence is acceptable as the subject *(I)* is the same in both clauses.

4 Participle clauses are more common in writing than in spoken language.

didn't need to / needn't have

We use *didn't need to* and *needn't have* to talk about the necessity of past actions. There is a subtle difference between the two structures.

1 *Didn't need to* usually suggests that we didn't do something because it wasn't necessary.
*We **didn't need to** call an ambulance because he wasn't hurt badly. (= We didn't call the ambulance.)*
*He **didn't need to** book a hotel because it wasn't the holiday season. (= He didn't book a hotel.)*

2 *Needn't have* means that we did something but actually it wasn't necessary.
*We **needn't have** put on sun lotion because it rained all day. (= We put on sun lotion but it wasn't necessary because it rained all day.)*
*She **needn't have** worried because the test was really easy. (= She worried about the test but it wasn't necessary because the test was easy.)*

Unit 13

Passive report structures

1   We use passive report structures when we want to report information and the agent is not important.
    *Chinese **is thought to be** the most spoken language in the world. (= It is not important to say who thinks this.)*

2   We commonly use passive report structures with verbs such as *say, think, believe, know* and *consider*.

3   If we use a passive report structure to talk about beliefs or knowledge in the present, we use *to be* + past participle of the reporting verb + infinitive.
    *He **is believed to be** the last man who speaks this language.*
    *English **is known to have** an extremely large vocabulary.*

4   If we use a passive report structure to talk about beliefs or knowledge in the past, we use *to be* + past participle of the reporting verb + *to* + present perfect.
    *He **is thought to have spoken** more than 12 languages. (= He is dead.)*
    *They **are said to have been** a highly sophisticated tribe. (= The tribe no longer exists.)*

5   Passive report structures are quite formal and are more commonly used in news reports than in spoken language.

Unit 14

Clauses of purpose: *to / in order to / so as to*

1   When we want to give the reason why someone did something, we can use a number of different linking words, e.g. *to, in order to* and *so as to*.
    *We arrived early **in order to** get a good seat.*
    *I phoned him **to** cancel the appointment.*
    *I told him about my problems **so as to** help him understand.*

    NB *to* is less formal than *in order to* and *so as to*.

2   When we want to make these sentences negative, we put *not* before *to*.
    *He didn't tell me too much **so as not to** spoil the film for me.*
    *I didn't say anything **not to** disappoint them.*
    *We left early **in order not to** get there too late.*

Result clauses with *so / such (that)*

1   We use *so / such (that)* to show how one thing is the result of another thing.

2   We use *so* with an adjective or an adverb.
    *He spoke **so quickly (that)** I didn't understand a word he said.*
    *The film was **so bad (that)** we left before the end.*

3   We use *such* with a noun.
    *It was **such an interesting film (that)** I thought about it for days.*
    *They are **such boring people (that)** I'd be happy never to see them again.*